*Search for the Absolute
in Neo-Vedanta*

Search
for the Absolute
in Neo-Vedanta

K.C. Bhattacharyya

*edited and with
an Introduction by*
George Bosworth Burch

The University Press of Hawaii
Honolulu

The Introduction was previously published as "Search for the Absolute in Neo-Vedanta: The Philosophy of K.C. Bhattacharyya" in *International Philosophical Quarterly* (December 1967).

"Place of the Indefinite in Logic," "The Subject as Freedom," and "The Concept of the Absolute and Its Alternative Forms" were previously published in G. Bhattacharyya, ed., *Studies in Philosophy*, vol. 2 (Calcutta: Progressive Publishers, 1958).

Library of Congress Catalog Card Number 75-17740

ISBN 0-8248-0296-9

Manufactured in the United States of America

Designed by Penny L. Faron

Contents

Foreword

The final editing of the manuscript was undertaken after the death of George Burch in 1973 by Professor Robert E. Carter, Trent University, Canada, former student, friend, and philosophical colleague. The index was prepared by Miss Margaret Jacobs under his direction.

Preface

The three essays reprinted here are the central works of the three phases in the development of K. C. Bhattacharyya's philosophical thought, in which he defines the Absolute as Indefinite, as Subject, and as Alternation respectively. "Place of the Indefinite in Logic" was published at Serampore in 1916. "The Subject as Freedom" was a series of lectures delivered at the Indian Institute of Philosophy at Amalner in 1929. "The Concept of the Absolute and Its Alternative Forms" was the Presidential Address at the 1933 meeting of the Indian Philosophical Congress. All were reprinted in the second volume of K. C. Bhattacharyya's collected works published at Calcutta in 1958.

The Introduction appeared in the *International Philosophical Quarterly* of December 1967 under the title "Search for the Absolute in Neo-Vedanta: The Philosophy of K. C. Bhattacharyya."

I am indebted to Professor Gopinath Bhattacharyya, editor of the collected works, for permission to reprint the essays, and to Professor W. Norris Clarke, S.J., editor of the *International Philosophical Quarterly*, for permission to reprint the Introduction.

G. B. B.

Introduction

Search for the Absolute is the central concern of Vedanta philosophy.[1] All sources of knowledge—reason, revelation, experience[2]—are employed for its speculative apprehension, and all ways of spiritual progress—doing, loving, knowing—are utilized for its practical attainment. The monist or non-dualist *(advaita)* school of Vedanta philosophy differs from the other schools (dualist, qualified non-dualist, and dualistic non-dualist) in that search for the Absolute is its exclusive concern, all else being rejected as illusion. In this school practical philosophy is based strictly on knowing and speculative philosophy, conceived as the rational analysis of ordinary experience, is based strictly on reason. The Absolute is sought in experience, not in analysis of abstract being, but it is sought by means of reason. The authority of the revealed Upanishads is accepted only in the sense of faith seeking understanding, a clue and psychological aid to truth but not a dogmatic basis from which to infer it. The possibility of mystical experience is admitted as of merely religious, not philosophical or cognitive, significance. *Moksha*, ineffable intuition of the Self as Absolute Reality, transcends reason to be sure, but it also transcends philosophy, to which it is related, if at all, as an end to which philosophy may be a means. Non-dualist Vedanta, therefore, is to be evaluated on rational grounds alone. Rejection of revelation or skepticism concerning mysticism is irrelevant. And if reason is universal, any validity non-dualism

may have is likewise universal, nowise conditioned by or confined to the Hindu culture in which historically it developed.

In the classical tradition of non-dualist Vedanta, represented
for example by Yajnavalkya in prehistoric, Gaudapada in ancient, Shankaracharya in medieval, Prakashananda in modern,
or Malkani in contemporary times, a consensus has developed
that the phrase *being-consciousness-bliss* (*sat-chit-ananda*) is the
most adequate formula for describing the Absolute (*Brahman*)—it
being understood that this is not literally a description of the
ineffable Absolute but a way of thinking of it in our human
concepts. The neo-Vedanta which has arisen in the twentieth
century, while not denying the correctness of this formula, is not
satisfied with merely repeating or deducing it. It strives to find
ever more adequate concepts for describing the Absolute, not as a
goal to be achieved (only *moksha* is the goal) but as progress in the
interminable search for understanding. Neo-Vedanta has developed in the favorable cultural environment formed by the
struggle for political independence, the religious revivals of the
Ramakrishna Order and Brahmo-samaj, and the Bengali literary
renaissance. Its teachers are university professors writing in English, the language of education and scholarship in modern
India. Neo-Vedanta is not a doctrine to be accepted or rejected
but a way of thinking capable of indefinite development and
variation, a lively shoot on the ancient stock of Vedanta
philosophy.

The protagonist of neo-Vedanta philosophy[3] is Krishna
Chandra Bhattacharyya (1875-1949), King George V Professor of
Mental and Moral Philosophy in the University of Calcutta.[4]
Students of his philosophy, even those who reject his doctrines
(notably the editor of his works, II:vi) or positively oppose them
(notably G. R. Malkani, whose *Vedantic Epistemology* includes a
penetrating criticism), are impressed by the subtlety, profundity,
and suggestiveness of his thought. While definitely within the
tradition of non-dualist Vedanta, it is informed by his original
genius[5] and also enriched by influences from non-Vedantic
philosophy both Indian and Western, influences however in
which the non-Vedantic accretions (and the same can be said for
the Vedantic core also) are so reinterpreted as to transform rather
than merely incorporate the philosophical content. But no com-

prehensive study of his philosophy has been published.[6] Besides
the intrinsic difficulty of following the subtle dialectic there are
certain extrinsic difficulties.

Unavailability of texts is no longer a difficulty since the publication of K. C. Bhattacharyya's philosophical works, published and
unpublished,[7] under the title *Studies in Philosophy* (Calcutta:
Progressive Publishers, vol. I, 1956; vol. II, 1958), edited by his
eldest son Gopinath Bhattacharyya, the present incumbent of his
father's chair as King George V (now called Brajendranath Seal)
Professor at Calcutta. References in this Introduction are to volume and page of that edition [see note 2]. All his works are short
and concise: the two most important articles, "The False and the
Subjective" and "Concept of the Absolute and Its Alternative
Forms," are of 7 and 18 pages respectively; the only books he
published, *Studies in Vedanta* and *The Subject as Freedom*, are of 79
and 73 pages; unpublished lecture series on Kant, Sankhya, and
Yoga are of 48, 76, and 105 pages; the two volumes of twenty-one
works and their analyses total 720 pages.

The brevity of Bhattacharyya's works does not imply that they
can be read quickly. The principal difficulty in studying his
philosophy is the austerity of his written style. He out-Kants
Kant and out-Hegels Hegel, his favorite Western philosophers,
in incomprehensibility. He uses only common words, but he uses
them with precision, saying exactly what he means, with no
figures of speech, rhetorical embellishments, or simplifications,
and the reader unaccustomed to such literary severity is
psychologically unprepared to grasp the meaning.[8] He realized
the difficulty of his writings, but said they were clear to him, and
he did not expect others to be interested in his ideas.[9] Still, while
difficult, it is not impossible to understand them: the trick is to
fathom the sentence structure, locate the antecedents of the pro-
nouns, and have faith that what is stated is exactly what is
intended.

Further difficulty results from apparent inconsistencies, but I
cannot find any real inconsistencies or that he ever retracted a
previous statement. Bhattacharyya's philosophy is not a
system[10] but a living organism of thought into which new material is assimilated, never raw but digested by interpretation, and in
which the same form becomes ever different as it develops under

the impetus of an intellectual vital force. The phases of his thought are alternative rather than exclusive formulations of his philosophy. The concept of alternation itself as a logical and metaphysical category is perhaps his most original contribution to philosophy, although he attributed it to Jainism, and the study of its development is of special interest. The phases of his thought cannot be confined in chronological periods; the article on Jainism is separated from the associated article on the Absolute and its alternative forms by a decade of works belonging to another phase; the lectures on Kant were written long after the papers of the Kantian phase; and the dominant concept of each phase can also be found in the others. Only by a distinction of phases, however, can the various aspects of his thought be integrated and its organic character appreciated.

To define the Absolute was his idea from beginning to end. In the first phase of his philosophy he defines the Absolute as *Indefinite*, in the second phase[11] as *Subject*, in the third phase as *Alternation*.

First Phase: The Absolute as Indefinite

In his first phase K. C. Bhattacharyya defines the Absolute as Indefinite in accordance with the Upanishadic doctrine that *Brahman* or *Atman* is best described negatively as *neti neti* ("not that, not that").[12] Vedanta was in his blood. Taught by his grandfather, a pandit who observed the brahmanical rites but also fraternized with missionaries to whom he taught Sanskrit, Krishna Chandra was raised in an atmosphere, as Kalidas Bhattacharyya puts it, of "alternation between orthodoxy and liberalism." As a child he had faith in the shastras, the Hindu philosophical classics. He studied Western philosophy at Presidency College in Calcutta, but his temper remained Vedantic. He had no personal guru, saying that the shastras are the guru. But while he had faith in the Upanishads and shastras, he maintained that faith in any scripture implies that the believer should raise himself to the writer's standpoint and feel the truth as the writer felt it. To understand what he believed was the central concern of his life. A Premchand Roychand scholarship[13] had for its thesis his first book, *Studies in Vedantism* (1904, published 1907).

Traditional Vedanta

This book gives the author's original interpretation of the non-dualist Vedanta which is the basis of his speculation. It presents, he says, "a metaphysical view which is dimly traceable in the Upanishads and which can hardly be said to have been completely brought out even by the commentators" (I:31). It is, he seems to mean, what the Upanishads and Shankara would have said had they thought it through. Still, the traditional doctrines are there. The self, only to be characterized as *neti, neti* (I:25), is nonetheless described, in the revealed "central truth of the Vedantic system," as undifferenced "being, consciousness, and bliss" (I:69). Wherever there is identity in difference, "the identity is the truth and the difference is illusory" (I:38). All perception is illusory (I:73), and the phenomenal world is unreal (I:81). But there are two sides to the Vedantic doctrine of illusion: the world is "unreal apart from *Brahman* and real in the reality of *Brahman*"; the latter side, he adds, "is frequently overlooked" (I:43). And it is just this transcendental realism, the obverse of the empirical subjectivism, which makes revelation necessary for knowledge. "If it be granted that spirit can only teach spirit and that truth can only be *recognised* and not created by mental activity, it must also be granted that revelation is necessary, and that the Word is God, and that accordingly there should be an eternal succession of omniscient teachers" (I:69). It is reason, however, which enables the mind to comprehend these truths and so prepares the way for their intuitive realization (I:70).

The concept of alternation, so important in Bhattacharyya's later thought, already occurs in this early work, in a cosmic, a metaphysical, and an epistemological context. (1) Creation and dissolution succeed each other in time: creation is the function of God as action (Brahmā); dissolution, that of God as unconsciousness (Siva); subsistence of the world, that of God as providence (Vishnu). "The alternation of the Trinity is eternal: it is only the nothingness of *Karma* artistically exhibited on the stage of time"—emanation from God's point of view, evolution from ours (I:60). (2) God (*Ishvara*) and the Absolute (*Brahman*) are the same in denotation but different in connotation (like a sphere of light viewed from circumference or center respectively). The Upanishadic verse "May I pass from the dark blank to the figured determinate and from thence to the blank again" indicates "this mystic scintillation of the One reality" in its indefinite and definite aspects, the "conceived inconceivability" which is the "ultimate formula" (I:50). (3) Ignorance and the evil will of which it is "the intellectual reflex" (I:52) are due to partial original sin or irrationality explicable only by preexistence (I:55). Ignorance is not necessarily overcome by the "wonderful power of the understanding," as Hegel held, because at every step dialectical thought, "necessary as it is, has the alternative of absolute scepticism beyond it" (I:53).

Two other works, written much later for special occasions, are also concerned with his interpretation of traditional Vedanta. "Shankara's Doctrine of Maya" was Bhattacharyya's contribution to the first session of the Indian Philosophical Congress in 1925. The fact of illusion (*maya*), like the fact of the Absolute (*Brahman*), cannot be established by reason. When believed by faith in revelation or suggested by the feeling of the vanity of life, however, it can then be interpreted by thought and be seen to be rationally intelligible (I:95). The experience of dissipation of illusion gives meaning both to illusion and to reality. "The quality of reality is explicitly felt only when it is experienced as dissipated in an illusion" (I:96). But non-dualist Vedanta denies reality to that which is not yet dissipated, that is, the world. "The acosmism of Shankara goes beyond both realism and idealism by reducing the world to absolute illusion, by interpreting the vanity of life as implying the denial of all given reality," while truth, on the other hand, is thought of "as utterly ungiven, i.e., as self-luminous" (I:96).

Illusion, analyzed in terms of the classic analogy of the rope mistaken for a snake, involves three stages: "the snake is first presented, it is next corrected, and then it is contemplated as corrected" (I:96)—and it is thus that the world appears "to uncritical thought, critical thought, and faith" (I:100). (1) The presentation of the unreal world can be thought of "as magic, as freedom, and as nought" (I:101), but it can be understood only as the opposite of dissipation, "the reversed process of the retractive freedom," God's "freedom to create or put forth as also to destroy or retract objectivity" (I:100). This is metaphysical subjectivism and epistemological realism. The world is illusion, existing only in our consciousness, but we are not introspectively aware of constructing it as we construct images. We see it because it is *there*, although not *really* there, "implicitly real" rather than merely "unreal" (I:99). As he says elsewhere, "objects exist as distinct from the knowing of them," and "relation of objects is not a mere mode of knowing them but is as objective as the terms" (II:245). (2) Correction or dissipation of the cosmic illusion and corresponding knowledge of the real Absolute leave the world as still given but unreal, like the snake referred to a definite place where it is not (I:102). The objective illusion is corrected, but not the "subjective defect through which it is still given" (I:102), and until this "scandal" to reason is removed, absolute truth "is only conceived but not known." This is the "Kantian impasse" (I:104). (3) At the third stage the world is neither real nor unreal but indescribable. For some Vedantists this third stage is *jivanmukti* (final freedom from illusion although not from individual existence); the world is indescribable at the second stage and simply disappears at the third, offering no problem. For Bhattacharyya, however, while *jivanmukti* may be attained at the second stage, the indetermination to which the world is reduced at the third still offers a problem. The world, now seen not to exist and never to have existed, is no longer a possible subject of which anything, even non-existence, can be predicated (I:98). It is neither existent nor non-existent, whereas the unreal object of the second stage was both existent and non-existent. The indescribable world, however, cannot be ignored. It "should be nought but is still given in absolute mockery of thought" (I:99), marking the limit of thought and frontier of faith. The indefinite Absolute, on the other hand, is now apprehended not as *real*, which is known only in contrast to something unreal, but as *true*, which is known directly (I:101), not logically thought, "the self-evidencing truth" (I:106).

Bhattacharyya's second favorite word, after *alternation*, is *demand*. [14] The feeling of the vanity of life is accompanied by "the *demand* [15] for absolute certitude"; and the whole doctrine of illusion is a "formulation of this feeling and demand" (I:95). This is the key to overcoming agnosticism. For Kant absolute truth is unknown and unknowable. For Vedanta it is unknown, or rather "known as unknown," but for that very reason "*demanding* to be known" (I:104). Faith that this *demand* will be actualized is the basis of metaphysical knowledge. That which truly is *demands* to be known and must be known.[16]

The religious aspect of Vedanta, explicitly excluded from the work just discussed, is treated in the chapter "The Advaita and Its Spiritual Significance" contributed to *The Cultural Heritage of India* published in 1936. Here the emphasis is on the illusoriness not of the world but of the individual self—"the central notion of Advaita Vedanta" (I:113). The individual, mistakenly thinking that he is not free, needs a discipline which "will lead him to realize that his bondage is an illusion and that he is eternally free," and this discipline is primarily cognitive, not active or emotive (I:118), although these other paths also have a place in the full religious life.

Influence of Hegel

The principal non-Vedantic influence in the first phase was that of Hegel, whose system was accepted by many in Bengal at that time as the ultimate philosophy. Bhattacharyya was enamored of Hegel, but with reservations, and in his own way. He did not write any systematic work on Hegel, but we may presume that his interpretation of Hegel was no less original than that of Vedanta, Kant, or Jainism. Hegelian logic, he says, while it "does not admit the indefinite but holds instead that dialectic necessity is creative," does not actually create the new category the necessity of which it sees; the demand for a non-empirical method is recognized but not satisfied (II:211). This inability to create is, however, an "*implicit* admission of the indefinite" (II:231). It would seem that Hegel, like Shankara, stated implicitly what Bhattacharyya states explicitly.

Logic of the Indefinite

He is not original, of course, in maintaining that the Absolute, since it is not limited and therefore not definite, is indefinite. But how can the indefinite be defined? Christian theology has its affirmative and negative theology describing the ineffable God positively but figuratively or literally but negatively. The former would be unthinkable for Bhattacharyya, who never speaks figuratively; there is hardly a figure of speech in his collected works. And the latter would be equally unsatisfactory; his concern is to understand the Absolute, not to glorify it by rhetorically denying its limitations. In his last published work he does say that the Absolute "is only negatively understood . . . speakable only by way of symbolism . . . expressible only by the negation of *I* . . . by what I am not . . . not literally expressible at all" (II:116). But this is very different. Symbol is not metaphor. Affirmative theology predicates all positive attributes of God metaphorically, but this doctrine admits one precise symbol, the self or subject indicated by *I*, which applies literally to reality or self but symbolically to the Absolute which transcends even self, "believed in but not understood either in the objective or in the subjective attitude." Negative theology denies all attributes of God, but this doctrine denies only *I*; the positive character of the Absolute "is expressible *only* by the negation of *I*." This has little in common with the notion of *ineffable* as used in mystical literature for what can be experienced emotionally but not described in words.

Defining the indefinite is a logical problem. To elaborate traditional logic, which deals only with the definite, into a more complete system which has in it a place for the indefinite is the purpose of the article "Place of the Indefinite in Logic" in the *Calcutta University Silver Jubilee Volume* of 1916, the most important work of the first phase. It might seem to be merely a three-valued logic, with the indefinite "a third category side by side with affirmation[17] and negation" (II:232), like the three-valued logics developed by Reichenbach and others to handle the data of nuclear physics, but it is rather different. The purpose of Reichenbach's logic is to save the appearances; that of Bhattacharyya's is to save the reality. It is a dynamic dialectic, differing from Aristotle's logic not like Reichenbach's but like Hegel's, by which in part it was inspired.

A preliminary approach to the problem is made in the paper "Some Aspects of Negation" (1914). In all phases Bhattacharyya identifies reason with negation: affirmation is a dead form useless for deduction; negation is a living form by which something is drawn from something else; negative attention "is the very heart of all mental process" (II:211). This paper endeavors to show that "there are certain ultimate modes of logical thought" embodying incommensurable types of negation: (1) mere negation leaves the negated as rejected without any relations and so indefinite; (2) the negated as coordinate with the affirmed is equally definite; (3) affirmation is defined by negation, since each affirmation is "constituted by an infinity of differences, by infinite negation" (II:209); (4) since *any* particular may spring "from the vortex of negation," particulars must be "accepted as they come," with their ground inexplicable. In these four views being "is progressively reduced to negation"; in the last, "being is abolished and absolute negation alone remains, not only as inexplicably definite but also as "inexplicably self-related or self-negating, i.e., as a free function or activity" (II:210). The abstract types of negation are interpreted concretely as modes of illusion: (1) illusion, understood through its own negation as illusion of illusion, is subjectively opposed to self-identity; (2) the subjective idea, while not objective, still has its own definiteness and relations, distinct from the system of objects; (3) the illusion is taken as identity of objective given and subjective explanation—"the last thinkable affirmation which alternates with negation" (II:216); (4) the synthesis of mutual negations produces only uncertainty as to whether all particularity is illusion, and in this last mode the absence of all positive knowledge makes us aware of the unknown as what alone is not illusory. These types of negation indicate different philosophical temperaments, and all philosophical dispute is a conflict between them (II:207). Pragmatism, the resolution of truth into will, recognizes the fourth type, "creative negation," but, like Hegelianism, proposes no technique for attaining its goal of constructing truth. A discipline of negation is needed.

In "Place of the Indefinite in Logic" Bhattacharyya remarks that the indefinite has often found a place in metaphysics but has had none in logic, which should be neutral and applicable to any metaphysics. Logic is an objective science dealing abstractly with the forms of all thinkables—objective, subjective, or absolute. The most abstract and comprehensive distinction is that between the definite and the indefinite (II:227). This distinction is expressed in the principle that "the indefinite is not and is indefinite at once" (II:228) or that "the indefinite and definite are and are not one"

(II:233). In the analogous Hegelian synthesis of being and non-being the identity of the opposed terms is stressed, but in this principle identity and difference are equally stressed, the line between definite and indefinite being itself indefinite. The principle reveals the inadequacy of the three traditional forms of Western logic: against dialectic, it points to unreason as an alternative to reason; against formal logic, it suggests the indeterminate form of doubt or ignorance beyond determinate affirmation and negation; against empirical logic, it points out that the positive object of experience is "a determination carved out of the indeterminate" (II:229).

With regard to *terms*, the bounds demarcating them from the surrounding indefinite are themselves indefinite, and the term may be indifferently taken as either being or transition. With regard to *judgments*, the negation of the indefinite is indifferently affirmative or negative, hence the distinction between affirmative and negative is indefinable and "contradiction is just as conceivable as otherwise" (II:229). With regard to *inferences*, the alternation of the dynamic and static aspects in dialectic shows that "reason is indefinite in its very constitution" (II:230n). These and other considerations are elaborated in the article in ways which are sometimes difficult[18] to follow. With reference to *terms*, "the determinate *this* has not simply being and negation in its constitution but also the indefinite" (II:230), and either being or non-being or the indefinite can be taken as the starting point of logic. With reference to *judgments*, the relation may be taken alternatively as constituting its terms or not, and either affirmation or negation may be taken as prior to the other. With reference to *inferences*, as opposed to Hegelian logic (*therefore* taken "as the self-creating dialectic of truth"), empirical logic (*therefore* taken as the particular affirmation contingently reached through other particular affirmations), or formal logic (*therefore* taken as the explication of an affirmation by negation), this logic holds that the conclusion is "a definition of the indefinite matter to which reasoning has reference" (II:231). The given analytic necessity within the ideal inferential form is "somehow applicable to the indefinite matter of experience," and on the other hand "the synthetic material process is a definite necessity inexplicably emerging out of the indefinite" (II:232).

This logic, unlike the traditional ones, has categories applicable to widely different metaphysical and epistemological theories, including the Vedantic assertion of the unreality of the world. We must reject the dogmatic assumption that "the knowing self ought to move toward more and more determinate truth." The logical impulse may be satisfied "in getting rid of the limitation of the definite, and not in securing increase of definiteness" (II:239). So far as logic is concerned, freedom or the absolute state may be attained either in the direction of the definite or in that of the indefinite. The limiting mystery of philosophy is neither the definite nor the indefinite but their disjunction (II:239).[19]

Logic alone cannot establish the Absolute as the Indefinite. This is established by revelation. But logic can make it intelligible, provided the logic includes the category of *indefinite*. Logically, the term is a determination carved out of the indeterminate. Metaphysically, the definite object of experience is somehow defined out of its indefinite ground, which is itself never given in experience. "Relation must be between two definite terms" (II:247). The indefinite cannot be related, cannot be either subject or predicate of a judgment, is not relative to anything. This, however, is mere logic, and is not advanced as an ontological proof for the existence of the indefinite Absolute. At most, it shows (and that by a dubious conversion) that the Absolute, if there is any such thing, is indefinite. The existence of the Absolute is a presupposition accepted by faith. The purpose of neo-Vedanta is to understand the Absolute, not to determine whether it exists,[20] and it is understood paradoxically as what cannot be understood, the Indefinite, at once indefinite (not intelligible) and definite (yet somehow intelligible), "only negatively understood" (II:116).

Neo-Vedanta, however, like classical Vedanta, cannot remain satisfied with this quasi-negative conclusion, but seeks, if not any definite connotation, at least a definite denotation for the Absolute. The logical approach gives way to a psychological approach. Vedanta philosophy has always had an epistemological bias. It thinks of metaphysics not as the rational analysis of being but as the rational analysis of experience. The Absolute, as indefinite, cannot be any object of experience, but as the ground of all objects it is understood as the subject of experience. The Indefinite, remaining at every level of experience as a fringe not realized but demanding to be realized, is approached by gradual inward realization of the subjective. This brings us to the second phase of Bhattacharyya's philosophy, where the absolute Indefinite is interpreted as the absolute Subject.

Second Phase: The Absolute as Subject

In his second phase K. C. Bhattacharyya defines the Absolute as Subject in accordance with the Upanishadic formula *Tat tvam asi* ("You are it").[21] The Subject is analyzed in his second book *The Subject as Freedom* (lectures at the Indian Institute of Philosophy in 1929, published 1930)[22] and related logical problems are treated in a series of four articles written and published between 1927 and 1932.

Influence of Kant

The principal non-Vedantic influence in this phase was that of Kant. His interpretation of Kant, based on a thorough study of the texts in translation and formulated in a series of lectures delivered at Calcutta in 1935, is highly original.[23] Unlike the *objective reasoning* of science or ordinary philosophy, where the sequence of conclusion from data is taken as a fact independent of the reasoner's mind, Kant's *transcendental reflection* has its conclusion realized in the very consciousness of the reasoning (II:359). In such transcendental reflection "the free self alone is known to be real and the object is known to be phenomenal" (II:306). Kant's most important thesis, Bhattacharyya says, is "the transcendental ideality of time or the mental world, implying a distinction between self and mind" (II:304). By this, I take it he means: Kant's metaphysics is dissociated from the Augustinian-Cartesian dualism of mental self and material world as real substances and affiliated to non-dualist Vedanta, for which mind and matter are equally illusory as contrasted with the real self.

The three critiques, he insists, must be taken together, but the second is crucial. The conception of apriori knowledge in the first is connected with the moral apprehension of freedom in the second (II:303). Although space is known before time (II:324), the phenomenality of space is dependent on the phenomenality of time, and the latter is dependent on practical knowledge of the self as free causality (II:307). The object is known practically as "an emanation of the self as freedom" (II:305), but the *spatio*-temporal world is known theoretically as distinct from the self and so implying an unthinkable thing-in-itself, and this contradiction in the object as emanation of self yet not mere idea is resolved in aesthetic consciousness into a self-subsistent value (II:306). Causality, on the other hand, is inapplicable to mental phenomena; time is symbolized by space, and the permanent mind cannot be pictured but is only symbolized by the spatial world as gathered up in body[24] ("a point which Kant did not bring out"), hence only the external, not the mental, world is "heuristically imagined or reflectively judged to be self-subsistent" (II:311). There is however a practical belief in mental causality bound up with the practical knowledge of free causality. Content of external object, emergence of mental object, and affection of the subject are one and the same fact, that is, sensation (II:315), which is the "conscious limit to free imagination" (II:313), something *positively limiting* the free act (II:314)—a suggestion of Bhattacharyya's crypto-realism as a clue to the maze of Kantian idealism.

This maze is followed through devious arguments which integrate the doctrines of the three critiques. Primarily, however, the transcendental philosophy is concerned with the transcendental or non-objective, that is, a content not distinct from the consciousness of it, which for Kant is *the self as conscious act of freedom* (II:301) realized through willing (I:285). This is the foundation and presupposition of the whole system. Even the Transcendental Aesthetic presupposes without proving a real self utterly unobjective; objective causality is intelligible only in reference to the self's free causality; and the conclusion that the self constructs the known object would be a mere figure of speech without prior theoretical knowledge of the self as real (II:304). Assuming the *subjective attitude,* that we do not know the self as object or mind, is the first, negative, step toward practical knowledge of the self as free cause (II:308). Self, to be sure, is mind, but mind is not self (II:313). Essentially the self is freedom. This is not indeterminism, for only *right* willing is free (II:343); there is no "bad freedom" (II:346). Good or free will knowing itself as free in the knowledge and as the condition of the moral law is Kant's "master principle" (II:347). This knowledge of the self or subject as freedom, which is the presupposition of Kant's transcendental philosophy, is the demonstrated conclusion of Bhattacharyya's *The Subject as Freedom.*

Epistemological Problems

Transcendental psychology, which is the theme of that book, is first defined two years earlier in the article "Knowledge and Truth" (read at the Indian Philosophical Congress in 1927, published 1928). Objective logic recognizes negation only as exclusion from a particular context. Epistemology recognizes negation as pure non-existence. But transcendental psychology, a sort of meta-epistemology, recognizes falsity, which is apparent existence, something we are aware of but do not know (II:151). A known content ("this is so") is not as such known as true, but only as implicitly true, "demanding" to be known as true (II:163). Only when it is challenged and confirmed ("I *know* that this is so") is it explicitly true. Now the truth, formerly fused with the content, is distinguished from it.[25] Knowledge and truth, therefore, imply each other: only truth is known, and only the known is true (II:154). Truth, thus distinguished from its content, is known as such, and as such is the ultimate reality present in all things.[26]

This affiliation of epistemology and metaphysics is developed more explicitly in the article "Fact and Thought of Fact" (1931). The coherence, correspondence, and pragmatic theories ("the characterization of fact as what stands in a constant system of relations or as what is given and not constructed by the mind or as what conditions and constitutes successful willing") are summarily rejected on the ground that they already assume some fact. *Fact* is defined as *what is believed:* "what a person believes is a fact to him" (II:169). The concepts *fact, thought, speakable, thinkable, assertable,* and *existent* are carefully distinguished and analyzed. Fact does not imply existence. Non-existence is also fact; the moral "ought," neither existent nor non-existent, is also fact—provided they are believed. But a fact is *thought* only when a question of existence is involved (II:170)—and the article is largely concerned with the defense of this existential thesis. A content abstracted from its possible existence is a significant speakable but has no objective meaning even as "subsistent." An *unreal* content may or may not have been previously believed, but it is *false* only if it was previously, but no longer, believed to be at least possibly existent (II:173). Here as always Bhattacharyya emphasizes negation, falsity, unreality. We advance in wisdom not by discovering new existences—existence is obvious and does not need to be discovered—but by discovering new non-existences, that is, by rejecting what we formerly thought to be existent.

These logical considerations form a framework[27] for Vedanta metaphysics. To deny subjectivity is meaningless, but to deny objectivity, to say an objective content is neither existent nor non-existent, is merely unthinkable. It is not meaningless to suggest that objectivity, including both existence and non-existence, is unreal. It is, to be sure, impossible and motiveless for *logic*. The suggestion acquires value only through a *spiritual* feeling or experience of such unreality—"a *spiritual* feeling of the symbolistic character of the object or of its unsubstantiality in itself or both, of the vanity of the object-interest as independent of the spiritual interest—the heart of religion and the perennial spring of all idealism" (II:175). But no question can arise about the facthood of the subject unless it is artificially objectified by language or otherwise, apparent doubt referring only to some symbolic characterization of it. The subject as spirit realizes itself on the one hand by freeing itself from objectivity, on the other hand by "contemplating itself as object to consolidate its freedom" (II:176). So long as the dualism of logical and spiritual consciousness persists, object is unquestioned, subject unquestionable, fact. Their unity, neither asserted nor denied by logic, is realized only when object is recognized as the spirit's symbolizing of itself.

Rasvihary Das summarized and criticized this article in a paper in the same journal.[28] He questioned especially the definition of *fact* as *what is believed* and the restriction of *thought* to *possible existents,* and he concluded that opponents of non-dualist Vedanta (like himself) should be grateful for the concession that the denial of objectivity is neither logical nor thinkable, so that those who do not utilize "any spiritual consciousness other than the logical or thinking one" need not admit it. Replying in the same number,[29] Bhattacharyya says that his definition indicates the use, not the linguistic definition, of *fact*. He reasserts and elaborates the thesis that to think is to think a content which is thought as a possible existent. Anything else, even though made up of meaningful elements, is only tried to be thought, not thought. Admitting that the article is slanted toward non-dualist Vedanta, he goes beyond his own text to say that *spiritual feeling* (of the world's unreality) is equivalent to *scriptural teaching*, that the ultimate unreality of the world fits in with the object's "indeterminate logical status," that this is like Kant's moral postulates' giving reality to his theoretic ideas, and that in Vedanta "logic follows faith or spiritual experience."

The thesis of the article just discussed, that a belief is false only if previously held, is both elaborated and qualified in an article, "Correction of Error as a Logical Process," four months later. Correction of error, disbelieving in what I am aware I believed, cannot be expressed in any unitary "logical form" (form referring only the content of thinking and not to the thinking itself). It requires two sentences: *"This* was taken as *this snake"* and *"What this* was taken to be was no fact"—sentences which cannot logically be combined into one (II:182). Correction cannot be formulated without referring to the past believing. The *present* consciousness, which is belief in *this* being a rope is not disbelief in *this snake,* because for it there is no such thing even to disbelieve. The content *this snake* was true[30] when the belief was there and is false in relation to the present belief (II:185).[31] There is no awareness of the content *this snake* as having been false when believed. What was then taken as *this snake* was not false, and what is now taken as false is not *this snake* (II:187). Correction "is not disbelieving in a previously believed *content* but only disbelieving that the previous belief had a content at all" (II:188). This view of a contentless belief, he claims, although "perilously near an idealistic view according to which object is nothing but belief with its subjectivity alienated," is, strictly speaking, realistic (II:189). Now that I disbelieve, I cannot describe in objective terms what I then believed, but neither can I say that there was only the subjective fact of contentless belief (II:190). The content is neither fact nor nothing.[32]

The discussion of correction of error is strictly abstract, but its metaphysical application is obvious. Rope is *Brahman,* snake the physical world, correction *moksha.* Theoretical denial of the world cannot be formulated in a single sentence because we cannot speak simultaneously from both points of view. Before *moksha* this world is experienced and believed. After *moksha* it is nothing. Perhaps we might, speaking figuratively, imagine *Brahman* as denying all possible worlds, but not this world (just as we might deny that there are any snakes in the jungle, but not that the snake we mistook the rope for is there). In our present state of illusion, however, the world is fact. If I see a rope as a snake, I can say truly, "This is a snake," whereas it would be a lie to say, for example, "This is a scorpion" (and equally a lie to say, "This is a rope"—as I might say to encourage a timid companion). Likewise, the world is fact so long as we see it, and it is fallacious either to deny its events theoretically or reject its demands practically on the ground of a hypothetical future enlightenment.

Falsity and Subjectivity

"The False and the Subjective" (1932), the last and most important of these four logical treatises, asserts the thesis that consciousness of the false and consciousness of the subjective imply each other. Whatever is false is reflected on, and whatever we reflect on is false. According to Professor T. R. V. Murti of Banaras Hindu University (who has been called the one among Bhattacharyya's students who best understood him), this is the basic principle of Bhattacharyya's philosophy.[33]

The first half of this thesis, that consciousness of the false is thereby consciousness of the subjective, is the less difficult to understand. It is a more explicit development of the doctrine of "Correction of Error as a Logical Process" that correction of error is disbelief in what we are conscious of having believed. Consciousness of the false is consciousness of a content speakable[34] only as the content of a belief which in turn is speakable only as "that the content of which is false" (II:195). Falsity is not mere objective non-existence, and disbelief is not mere lack of belief. Disbelief is a positive mode of consciousness, the correction or rejection of what was believed. The false is what is rejected or disbelieved, and can be expressed only as what was believed. What was believed is neither the *judgment* "This is A" (for the copula expresses only a confused unity of the fact believed and the believing act) nor the *proposition* "This being A" (for the copula expresses a relation between the terms, whereas the belief was in the concrete this as related to A) but the *content* "This as A" (the concrete fact this as characterized by A). But the content of the corresponding disbelief cannot be expressed in this form; we cannot say that "This as A" *was* believed, for the word *this* would mean content of a present belief. The content of disbelief can be expressed only as "what was believed," the *what* being unspecifiable in objective terms. The prior belief cannot be specified by its content, for the content is specified only by reference to it. The previous belief can be spoken of only in reference to the disbelief, can be specified only as that the content of which is false or disbelieved. Disbelief, consciousness of prior belief, is a form of non-cognitive consciousness (consciousness of something which cannot be spoken of without reference to the consciousness), *reflective* consciousness referring not to object but to itself, subjective. "To be conscious of the false as such," therefore, "is to be conscious of the subjective"(II:197).

The second half of the thesis, that consciousness of the subjective is thereby consciousness of the false, is more difficult to understand. It appears, as the author himself remarks, "paradoxical, if not obviously false" (II:197). The reader should realize, however, that Bhattacharyya means this very seriously, and should try to understand its significance.[35]

In the first place, "consciousness of a belief implies disbelief in its content" (II:197). Consciousness of *belief*, as contrasted with consciousness of its content, is not mere memory, not noncommittal consciousness of the content as merely subsistent, but is consciousness of having the past belief for present rejection or reaffirmation. To reject a belief is to dissociate its content from fact. To reaffirm a belief implies consciousness that the content might not be fact and so also is to dissociate the content from fact. But "we are conscious of the dissociation of the content from fact *only through positive disbelief* (II:199).[36] Reaffirmation is "the rejection of disbelief," so that consciousness of a past belief as true is also consciousness of its being false. In case of *doubt*, there is alternation of belief and disbelief. Whenever we are explicitly conscious of a past belief, we have a disbelief in its content. Reflection is always negative.[37] As he says elsewhere, "the appearance of presentation is a disbelieved possibility of object" (II:77).

In the second place, "consciousness of the subjective is consciousness of a belief" (II:199), of a content with intentional (believing or disbelieving) reference to fact. Introspection, reflective consciousness or consciousness of the subjective, is distinguishing the subjective, that is, a mode of consciousness, from its content. What we are reflectively conscious of is the consciousness of "a content as what is or may be believed" (II:200). Since consciousness of a belief involves disbelief in its content, consciousness of the subjective is consciousness of the false (II:201). Reflective consciousness involves disbelief in the content of the corresponding unreflective consciousness. We think reflectively only in order to reject some belief.

Bhattacharyya states, without discussing, two corollaries of this thesis: "the object is through the self-alienation of the subject," and "the subject is not known except by a denial of the object" (II:195). These may be rephrased to say that the object is relative to the subject, consequently *the Absolute is subject;* and that in its essence so far as it is knowable *the subject is freedom* from object. These are the central doctrines of the book *The Subject as Freedom.*[38]

Transcendental Psychology

This book is described[39] as "a systematic elaboration of the concept of subjectivity, conceived in general after Vedanta as conscious freedom or felt detachment from the object." The first two chapters (II:19-49) present abstractly the principles of *transcendental psychology,* and the remaining eight chapters (II:50-92) are its concrete application to the steps of subjectivity.

In an earlier work Bhattacharyya raised the question whether the antithesis between subjective and objective, which "has only been reached very gradually in the history of thought" (II:207), is a necessary dichotomy at all. Apparently he resolved this question in the affirmative, since this dichotomy is the fundamental category of thought in *The Subject as Freedom. Object* is whatever is *meant.* But that which is significantly speakable and communicable and even intelligible is not necessarily meant. *Subject* is not meant. The word *I* has no universal meaning, since its significance differs for each speaker; the thing intended, the speaker himself, is understood "through the word but not through the *meaning* of the word" (II:19, 26, 83, 85). Since *I* has no meaning, whereas *this* (symbolizing what is perceived) does, the statement *this is I* is rejected as false, but *I am this* is only felt as undeniable (II:20). *You* and *he* also indicate the subject, and the three persons are known neither to be distinct from nor to be identical with each other (II:23). Object is known (although not indubitably) as distinct from subject. Subject, however, is *known* (indubitably) in itself, although it is *felt* as dissociated both from object and from other subjects (II:23). Metaphysics, which studies "reality conceived as meanable" (II:24; cf. 27), is not concerned with the subject.

What is concerned with the subject is *transcendental psychology* (to be carefully distinguished from metaphysics, mysticism, epistemology, or introspective psychology), which studies knowing and subjective function in general by "the spiritual cultivation of a subjective attitude" (II:28). Consciousness of the subjective is consciousness of the false, rejection of object. This is a gradual process with several steps or modes. "The modes of subjectivity are the modes of freeing oneself from the modes of objectivity" (II:28). But transcendental psychology goes beyond this. It not only analyzes "the positively felt and believed freedom of the subject from objectivity" but also elaborates "modes of freedom that have no reference to object at all" (II:29). For metaphysics (objective attitude) the knownness of the object appears positive and knowing "its problematic negation," and the object appears to exist beyond its relatedness to the subject. For transcendental psychology (subjective attitude), of which Kant's critical philosophy is a disguised form,[40] freedom is positively believed, the objectivity of the object appears as not belonging to it (like change) but as the subject's self-negation, the transcendent object is meaningless, and metaphysics is "the quest of a chimera" (II:30).

Spiritual progress, realization of the subject as free, may result unselfconsciously from a good life, but for others theoretical elaboration of stages of freedom may propose a discipline for such realization. "Consciousness of perfection, freedom, or salvation" is a *demand* for activity which takes the form of dissociation of the subject from the object by theoretical "awareness of the subject as what the object is not" (II:32).[41]

The relatedness of an object to the subject, its knownness or feltness, studied in transcendental psychology in abstraction from the object itself, is called *psychic fact* (II:34).[42] Psychic fact is not coordinate with objective fact; it "should be more real but is actually less real" (II:47). It is only " in the awareness of the illusory" (II:39) and "as the implication of belief in value" (II:157) that the relatedness or presentation of the object emerges from the perceived object into which it was merged. This emergence is freedom which "no longer embodies belief" in the object. The object possesses knownness just as it possesses color, but the knownness, unlike the color,[43] can be studied independently and so reveals knowing as distinct from object known. Unlike objective fact, which is known as accomplished, psychic fact is known as being accomplished ("at once accomplished and to be accomplished"), a reality which "is only not denied as objective and may be conceived to be subjective" (II:42). In becoming known, however, it is converted into object, "a fact of which we are introspectively aware as capable of existing apart from introspection" (II:50). To the Kantian objection that "the metaphysical reality thus adumbrated in the presentation" is only subjective, though appearing real by a permanent illusion corrigible only in a moral or aesthetic way, Bhattacharyya answers that psychic fact demands to be known cognitively and that this demand can be fulfilled (II:43). A faith spiritually demanded (like Kant's moral postulates) must be capable of becoming knowledge (II:44). The reality behind the object, known as unknown, is not objective thing-in-itself, subjective in the sense of illusion, or unknowable content of faith, but the subject of which we become aware by its constructive faculty through which the object comes to be for the subject and its self-realizing activity through which it frees itself from the object (II:43).[44] The will to realize the self implies knowledge of the self as unknown but knowable and demanding to be known (II:44). As with Kant, although inaccurately interpreted by him,[45] will is the key to knowledge.

Modes of Subjectivity

There are three general modes or stages of subjectivity—bodily subjectivity, psychic subjectivity, and spiritual subjectivity

(II:33). Each comprises a number of subsidiary modes. Each subsidiary mode involves freeing yourself from the corresponding mode of objectivity by assuming the subjective attitude, and each in turn becomes objective when viewed from the objective attitude and so itself demands to be transcended.

Bodily subjectivity is that by which my body, although part of the physical world, is nevertheless dissociated from other perceived objects and identified with myself. An object may be present in any of three ways—as external, as internal, as absent (II:55)—environmental objects being in the first or third class, body in the first or second. Present external objects are purely objective, not distinguished from their presentation, and are perceived only as exteriors; their unseen sides are imagined as perceived by me from a different direction, and their invisible insides are imagined, if at all, as perceived, that is, as exteriors. The exterior of my body is also perceived, although in a unique way. Whereas other objects are here or there relative to me,[46] the body is always here, and its unseen sides are imagined only as perceived by somebody else. The interior of the body, however, is not only imagined[47] but also directly *felt*. As felt it is not distinguished from the body as perceived, but the perceived body is somehow distinguished from the felt body as something itself imperceptible.[48] Feeling of the body is not psychic fact, yet it is the potentiality of psychic fact, being the possibility, although not the actuality, of being dissociated from the objective body (II:52). In actual feeling we are not interested in withdrawing from the environment, although an interest derived from higher modes of subjectivity may suggest such withdrawal (II:53), and this possible detachment is the "first hint" of freedom (II:54). The approach to psychic fact is found in knowledge, by conscious non-perception, of absence as a present fact.[49] Here the consciousness is detached from the object. The absence is perceived, or strictly speaking non-perceived, not felt or imagined, but the object is not perceived. Non-perception may be of *absence* (for example, a familiar field from which a tree has been removed, now perceived as having something missing, but something unidentified) or of *the absent* (for example, a book we cannot find, although there is no particular place where it is not) (II:57). Perceived absence (that of the tree) is like the felt body, not

dissociated from what is actually perceived. The absent known by conscious non-perception (the book) has no locus, is free from space, but not from time (the present), and so is not fully dissociated from object (II:60), but it is partly so dissociated, and is a transitional stage to the fully psychic fact of imagination (II:60).

Psychic subjectivity involves psychic fact, in which knownness is distinguished from the known in introspection. Abstract knownness, however, emerges only with the positive awareness of what is unknown (II:63). Psychic subjectivity begins with imagination. *Image* is fact, but a different sort of fact from object, a "substantive something from which the object is distinct" (II:62).[50] External object is known as with position, perceived body is imagined to have position, felt body is known as with an unknown position, absence is not known to be with position, but image is known to be without position. Like absence, image has no locus, but unlike absence it has no time-position either, not even present absence, though time-position is not denied to it (II:64). We must reject "the current banality that psychic facts are only in time while objective facts are in both space and time" (II:65). Image has objective form but no objective position and no necessary time. Image is always incomplete, a form being formed, substantive and functional (II:67)—else it would be percept. The completed form which fulfills the forming is *idea* (II:68). Idea, however, may be dissociated from image, idea of object as not imaged but sought[51] to be imaged, conscious want of image (II:69). Contrasted to such pictorial thought is *thought* proper, the content of which is unpicturable yet meaningful and therefore object. Thought is about object, but of something unobjective about object. Unimaginability of content and consequent awareness of the impossibility of its objectivity involve complete detachment from objectivity (II:70). Thought is eternal, altogether dissociated from time. It is *about* object, but its content is characterized "as what the object is distinct from" (II:71). It is a psychic fact, but having an object is not pure subjective activity. As compared with pure subject it is "objective in its very dissociation from objectivity" (II:71), necessarily characterized as *what the object is not*.

Spiritual subjectivity begins with *feeling*. While thought is negatively unobjective, as dissociated from the object to which it

refers, feeling is positively subjective, without any reference to object (II:73). It is not distinguished from its unthought, un-meant, and unmeanable content (though the latter may, in the objective attitude, be distinguished from it), for the content is recognized as mere symbolizing, not really its content at all (II:74). "Feeling does not *mean* anything but itself" (II:75). It is freedom first from actual and finally from all possible thought (II:77). In the subjective attitude, up to the stage of thought, object appears alien to subject, but in feeling the subject is free from all meant content, which is reduced to mere symbolism. It is free, but not yet freedom itself (II:88). The feeling of not having a feeling, awareness of wanting a feeling, leads to *introspection*, complete dissociation from felt being, the pure knowing function (II:79), freedom itself, though still as a distinct individual (II:88). Introspection, defined in general as "the distinguishing of the presentation of an object from the object" (II:66), acquires a deeper connotation, in the case of feeling, as awareness of feeling being distinct in itself, not *from* anything (II:80). Introspection involves not merely conscious absence of meaning but conscious impossibility of meaning, pure subjectivity, not meant "even as unmeanable," since it presents no problem in meaning (II:83). It is the *I*, the self, self-revealing. To the speaker *I* means actual introspection, but to the hearer *I* means a *possible introspection* (II:84). The latter awareness is a mode of self-consciousness which goes beyond actual introspection. Awareness of a possibly intuited subjectivity beyond that actually intuited indicates the possibility of subjective illusion comparable to objective illusion and governed by the same law that consciousness of the subjec-tive is consciousness of the false. Awareness of a subjective mode as beyond introspective appropriation suggests an introspection that is not appropriative, that rejects the distinct *I* and all distinc-tion as illusory. This ultimate mode of subjectivity, eliminating the exclusive *I*, having not even subjective fact distinct from itself, is the absolute self (II:87).[52]

At each step of this anagogic path[53] the subjective attitude appears as a demand for freedom from the illusory (II:54). Elab-oration of these stages of freedom suggests the possibility "of realising the subject as absolute freedom, of retracting the felt positive freedom towards the object into pure intuition of the self" (II:33). At its final stage the subjective attitude appears as a "conscious spiritual demand" for intuition of the subject (that which is not meant but intended, or rather intends, by the word *I*) as absolute freedom, absolutely unobjective (II:88-90). This demand is not fulfilled in introspection either actual or possible, where it is only a possibility to be realized (II:89). I am not introspectively aware even of my actual introspection, which is not itself introspected. But in my introspection of feeling I am aware that the self from which the feeling is distinguished may transcend both actual and possible introspection, may be free even from this distinction between (my own) actual introspection and (others') possible introspection, may be completely de-individualized (II:92). This does not mean that the Absolute is indefinite—the doctrine of Bhattacharyya's first phase before the adoption of the subjective attitude, and perhaps the most profound conclusion possible in the objective attitude. The absolute self or subject, although de-individualized and free from all distinctness, is still definite and positive. In classical non-dualism, as interpreted by Bhattacharyya, where *moksha* is not "something to be reached or effected or remanifested" but is the self itself as essence of *Brahman*, "the self or the absolute is not a thing having freedom but is freedom itself" (I:118). And in transcendental psychology the self or Absolute, progressively known at each step as relative freedom from object, is this freedom. When all distinctness is transcended, the subject is not a distinct thing, even a free thing, but simply *freedom*.[54]

K. C. Bhattacharyya is not unique in asserting that the subject is freedom. The most distinguished of his contemporary philosophers in East and West said the same. Nishida said: "The true noetic intelligible Self is essentially individual and free; it is freedom itself."[55] Bergson said: "*La conscience est essentiellement libre; elle est la liberté même.*"[56] But Bhattacharyya asserted this thesis as the significant conclusion of an extraordinarily subtle and original dialectic, and the precision and conciseness of his style made it possible to include a wealth of dialectical detail in a short book.

There are, however, some difficulties, not merely stylistic but substantial.

(1) *Willing* enters in a very awkward way into the discussion of feeling. It is said to be coordinate with feeling (as if the train of

thought were here running on a double track). Feeling is dissociation from objectivity, withdrawal from the object; willing is identification with objectivity, conquest over the object (II:75), conscious projection of objectivity (II:76). There is progress and regress[57] (as if the train of thought were backing up). The whole matter is passed over hastily. One might expect will to play a dominant role in the philosophy of freedom, just as it does in Kant's philosophy as interpreted by Bhattacharyya, but the psychological act of willing does not seem to have any place, at least any neat place, in the system.

(2) A still more basic difficulty is the identification of truth with freedom. Since consciousness of the false is consciousness of the subjective, we attain subjectivity or freedom, and ultimately absolute freedom, by progressive rejection of the false or illusory in favor of the true or real. The method is cognitive; the end, freedom, is presumably truth. That *the truth shall make you free* is a venerable principle, but is it really so? Does not devotion to truth require rather the sacrifice of freedom? Is not the first principle of scientific method to accept whatever evidence and logic show to be true regardless of what we may will? That truth is freedom is at best a paradox.

(3) A third difficulty may be suggested by the question, "Why assume the subjective attitude?" Granted it leads to freedom, is freedom an end which justifies the subjective attitude as a means, or is the subjective attitude somehow right in itself, with freedom a happy consequence justified by rather than justifying the means? Cannot a case also be made for the objective attitude?

Bhattacharyya does not discuss, or even raise, these difficulties. They are solved, however, by the concept of alternative forms of the Absolute which characterizes the third phase of his thought.

Third Phase: The Absolute as Alternation

In his third phase K. C. Bhattacharyya defines the Absolute as Alternation, in a departure from the Upanishadic tradition. The logical category of alternation, frequently appearing in his earlier works, is now applied to the Absolute itself. This is his most original contribution to philosophical thought.

Influence of Jainism

The principal non-Vedantic influence in this phase was that of Jainism.[58] About 1920 he studied and was impressed by the Jain philosophical work *Prameya Kamala Martanda*.[59] In the first chapter, after considering the various Indian schools of philosophy and discussing doubt and theories of error, the author presents his own theory of knowledge as that which reveals both itself and its object. In the second he refutes all absolutistic metaphysical theories in typical Jain fashion. In the third he discusses epistemological problems: memory, recognition, hypothetical argument, inference, causality, non-perception, authority. In the fourth he discusses the theories of relations and universals, distinguishing between continuant and recurrent universals (i.e., things and classes). In the fifth he considers what *appears* to be knowledge. In the sixth he analyzes the Jain categories of whole-expression *(sakaladesa)* and part-expression *(vikaladesa)* and defends the thesis that the former concerns ways of knowing *(pramanas)* and the latter concerns theories of philosophy *(nayas)*.[60]

Bhattacharyya's immediate reaction to this book was a paper "The Jaina Theory of *Anekanta*"[61] presented to his seminar at Dacca in 1921 (published 1925 in the first issue of the *Philosophical Quarterly*, reprinted 1943 in *Jaina Antiquary*), which introduces the third phase, although chronologically contemporary with the first. In analyzing *anekantavada* (non-absolutism), which is the Jain theory of truth, he affirms the category of alternation in the first sentence. "The Jaina theory of *anekanta* or the manifoldness of truth is a form of realism which not only asserts a plurality of determinate truths but also takes each truth to be an indetermination of *alternative* truths" (I:331). The purpose of the paper is to show the necessity of this "indeterministic extension" of ordinary realism, and that togetherness, the fundamental category of realism is itself manifold, signifying fundamentally different aspects of truth neither subsumed under a universal nor making a unity (I:332). The Jain category "distinction from distinction" has *alternative* values, only one of which is the togetherness of ordinary realism. We can think of a composite and its components alternatively but not simultaneously: if the former be given, the latter are *its* analysis; if the latter, the former is *their* plurality (I:332). Hegel subordinates distinction to identity, Nyaya (Hindu logic) subordinates identity to distinction, but Jainism makes them coordinate.

Jain logic, like Bhattacharyya's, involves the indefinite, which is thought and therefore objective. *Anekantavada* contrasts the difference between two definites with the difference between definite and indefinite, "and obtains from their contrast certain other forms of truth, simpler and more complex" (I:338). The objective, and therefore definite, indefinite, with these incompatible elements, is a togetherness of unrelated elements, neither one nor many, to be thought only as *alternation* (I:339). *Anekanta,* "the indeterminism or manifoldness of truth," appears primarily in the two forms of difference and non-difference, consecutive presentation and co-presentation.[62] The logical predicament of Jain logic, that "distinction from distinction is other than mere distinction and yet asserts the distinction" (I:339), is grounded in the epistemological predicament that the subject is distinct from the object yet knows the distinction (I:340). This "of-relation," the relation between knowing and content (no-content and content, no-being and being), is intelligible only by the category of indetermination. Distinction and identity (differenced and undifferenced togetherness, particularity and thinghood)[63] are related by *indetermination* or *alternation;* they are in each relation without being in the other relation at the same time. "Identity is distinct from distinction and yet implies it, i.e. is in *alternation* with it" (I:340).

Ordinary realism, he says, is based on the category of distinction; certain forms of realism, on distinction from distinction; Jain realism, on the indetermination of the two. This indetermination is developed into seven *alternative* modes of truth.[64] The definiteness of the given indefinite, which "sits lightly on the indefinite" as a detachable definite or affirmation with no existential import, is contrasted with characterless givenness or existence, its negation.[65] To say that a determinate existent A *is* in one respect and *is not* in another respect[66] "does not mean that A is A and is not B; it means that existent A, as existence universal, is distinct from its particularity"[67] (I:341). The determinate existent, therefore, is being and negation distinguishably together *(is and is not).* The indefinite, on the other hand, which involves non-distinction of being and negation, is neither not affirmed nor non-existent nor a distinction of affirmation and existence; it is a separate mode of truth, "indeterminate" *(avaktavyah)* (I:341). It is not expressible by any concept, but "a truth has to be admitted if it cannot be got rid of even if it is not understood" (I:342). The four modes of truth implied by the distinction between definite and indefinite are augmented by considering the indefinite either with or distinct from each of them. We thus complete the seven truth values of Jain logic, which Bhattacharyya describes as follows: particular affirmation, universal negation, affirmation and negation distinguishably together as determinate existent, the same indistinguishably together as indefinite, this indefinite as itself an affirmation, the indefinite as many negations together, the indefinite as distinct from the determinate existent. "These modes of truth are not merely *many* truths but *alternative* truths" (I:342). Each is *alternative* with the others, objectively possible. This is *indeterminism*, not of will but of cognition. What is presented is truth even though thinkable only in alternative ways (I:343).

This treatment of Jain logic is characteristically original. Bhattacharyya's interpretation of *anekantavada* (non-absolutism) is quite different from that of the Jain philosophers themselves, either classical or contemporary. Jain *anekantavada* means that in any given case each of the seven predicates (*is, is not,* etc.) may be asserted, not absolutely (for that would be to reject the others) but relatively, that is, somehow, in some respect (*syat*).[68] The purpose of research is not to determine the truth value for a given proposition but to determine the qualifications which must be specified to make each of the truth values apply. All are valid simultaneously (in different respects), not alternatively. The elephant inspected by blind men really and always is somehow like a wall, somehow like a column, somehow like a fan, somehow like a snake; it is not alternatively like a wall, a column, a fan, a snake. There is no skepticism in Jain logic (*syat* not meaning "maybe"), as Bhattacharyya correctly remarks (I:343), but neither is there alternation. What he calls Jain logic is not the logic of the Jains.

It is not to be supposed that Bhattacharyya mistakenly believed, through ignorance, that he was giving a historically faithful account of Jain teaching. Rather, he was showing, as Gopinath Bhattacharyya says, that "a *new* interpretation of the Jaina theory of *anekanta* is possible in the light of the concept of alternation" (I:xiv). In a postcard to Professor D. M. Datta dated

August 21, 1930, referring to this article, he wrote: "My paper was developed only in the general line of the doctrine of *syadvada*; if you take it as historical description of Jain philosophy, certainly there are many errors and defects there which you will easily understand."[69]

Nevertheless, Professor Kalidas Bhattacharyya of Visvabharati University, who has succeeded his father as the leading advocate of the theory of alternative forms of the Absolute, considers that this article does correctly interpret the Jain tradition. He says he cannot believe that the great Jain philosophers were teaching the trivial truism that there are different ways of looking at things. The *aneka* (not one) of *anekantavada* (non-one-end-ism) may have the negative meaning *not one* or the positive meaning *more than one*, so that *anekantavada* might mean "there is no one exclusive feature of reality" or "reality has many features." But incompatible features cannot be conjointly true; they alternate by not being exclusively true. *Anekanta* means not what is common in the seven modes, for they have nothing in common; not integration of the seven modes, for they cannot logically be integrated; but alternation among the seven modes, the only reasonable interpretation. Since it is the logically correct interpretation, we must assume that it is what the Jain logicians intended. Kalidas Bhattacharyya, if I understand him correctly, maintains that alternation is what the Jains must have taught, whereas his father maintained only that it is what they should have taught.

Be that as it may, K. C. Bhattacharyya interpreted Jain non-absolutism in the sense of alternation, statements each valid apart from the others but not in conjunction with each other. The attitude of alternation had always characterized his thought. It is found in his earliest works. It was fostered in his student days by uncertainty concerning Kant, Hegel, and Vedanta; sometimes he felt that Vedanta goes beyond Kant, sometimes that Kant goes beyond Vedanta. When he read the *Prameya Kamala Martanda,* he discovered in, or read into, Jain logic a systematic formulation of this attitude, and composed his paper on *anekanta*. At the first meeting of the Indian Philosophical Congress in 1925, the year the paper was published, G. Hanumanta Rao of Mysore presented a paper "The Jaina Instrumental Theory of Knowledge," in which he said: "Its [Jainism's] great defect lies in the fact that it yields to the temptation of an easy compromise without overcoming the contradictions inherent in the opposed standpoints in a higher synthesis."[70] Bhattacharyya, who was present at this meeting to read his own paper "Shankara's Doctrine of Maya" and may be presumed to have heard Rao's paper, would have agreed with this interpretation, similar to his own interpretation of Jain logic as alternation without integration, but for him this was its merit, not its defect. The concept of alternation developed in his own paper remained latent during his second phase, but emerged to dominate the thought of his third phase. It was in his interpretation of non-absolutism that he found the clue for comprehending the Absolute in a way at once more subtle and more profound than that given by the notions of Indefinite or Subject.

Consciousness and Content

The basic work of the third phase and final statement of Bhattacharyya's search for the Absolute is his Presidential Address at the 1933 meeting of the Indian Philosophical Congress, published in 1934,[71] entitled "The Concept of the Absolute and Its Alternative Forms." I say *final*, not *definitive*, as he never suggested, and I believe never supposed, that any philosophical statement is definitive. The Presidential Address, however, provided an appropriate occasion for a direct and explicit consideration of the central problem of philosophy, the nature of the Absolute. The ruling category of this address is taken from his interpretation of Jainism, but the content obviously reflects Kant's threefold critique, the vocabulary sometimes suggests Hegel, and the epistemological approach is characteristic of Vedanta. In his own copy the author marked paragraphs 2-4, 7, 15, 27-29, 31-41, and 44 with the letter O, and Gopinath Bhattacharyya suggests that O might have meant "omit" in anticipation of an abridged version. Taking this hint, I will base my summary primarily on the paragraphs not so marked.

"Philosophy starts in reflective consciousness." This first sentence of the address asserts Bhattacharyya's attitude toward philosophy. It needs no external motivation, either wonder as in the Western tradition or suffering as in the Hindu tradition. It is the natural activity of the human, "reflective," consciousness. Reflection is awareness of the relation between subject and object, consciousness and its content. "It is in reference to this relation that the concept of the absolute has to be understood" (II:125).

Within reflection consciousness and content are somehow distinct, yet their identity cannot be denied (II:126). Their relation is indefinite. But whatever appears as indefinite in some respect *demands* to be definable in that respect, and if such indefiniteness necessarily appears to a stage of consciousness, that stage demands a higher where the indefinite is defined (II:127). The demand is for a "supra-reflective consciousness" where the distinction of consciousness and content becomes clear. The concept of the Absolute belongs to such supra-reflective consciousness. It need not involve identity of consciousness and content. It is hypothetically understood within reflection simply as "a completely definite distinction of content and consciousness" (II:128).

It is already apparent that Bhattacharyya, if not actually rejecting, is certainly transcending the doctrines of his earlier phases. The logic of the indefinite is still required, but the indefinite as such is considered a challenge rather than a position, and the demand is for defining the Absolute, instead of conceding its apparent indefinability as ultimate. The search for the Absolute leads to a higher form of consciousness, that is, to "the Subject as Freedom," but the previously presupposed superior cognitive value of the subjective attitude is questioned, and the object or content, so ruthlessly condemned as illusory in the subject-oriented dialectic of that book, is now given its day in court. This is *anekantavada* in action.

Alternative Absolutes

There are three forms of consciousness: knowing, willing, feeling. The relation ("implicative distinction") between consciousness and its content (i.e., subject and object) is different in each form. In knowing the content is not constituted by consciousness; in willing the content is constituted by consciousness; in feeling the content constitutes "some kind of unity" with consciousness (II:129). Each, consequently, has its own "formulation of the absolute." For knowing, the absolute is *Truth*; for willing, it is *Freedom*;[72] for feeling, it is *Value*. The central thesis of Bhattacharyya's philosophy is that in reflective consciousness "these absolutes or formulations of the absolute" cannot be identified or integrated but are "in a sort of alternation" (II:128).

The content of *knowing* is not constituted by the knowing. "The particular act of knowing discovers and does not construct the object known." This is epistemological realism,[73] or rather a definition of what knowing means. *Knowledge* means "that the object known is in some sense independent of it." The subjectivism of *The Subject as Freedom* is now recognized as due to a confusion between knowing and willing. This realism, however, has two qualifications: (1) The object may essentially "be constructed by *some* knowing," although not by the particular act by which we know it. Metaphysical idealism *(mayavada)* does not imply epistemological subjectivism *(drishtisrishtivada)*;[74] we *know* something insofar as it *is* independently of the knowing, even if it *is* only as illusion. (2) What we ordinarily *claim* to know may be at least partly dependent on the knowing, but if so it is known only "empirically," not truly or absolutely (II:129).

The content of *willing* is constituted by willing; apart from the willing it is nothing. The willed future, unlike the known future, is not fact but contingency, not what will be but what would be if willed, not already determined but being determined by the willing.

The content of *feeling* is unified with the feeling. Feeling is consciousness of an imperfect distinction between content and consciousness. It is consciousness of *value*, which is as much content as consciousness, not both at once but each alternately. We do not know, but we cannot deny, that the value of an object is in it (II:130).

The known content, although before the mind only as known, is understood as distinct from knowing, not necessarily related to knowing (II:131). But this realist theory is true merely by definition; the significant question is, what, if anything, *is* known? What is known is eternal *truth;* the object may be temporal, but what is *known* about it is formulated in eternally true judgments (II:132). But contingent judgments ("It is to me") are not independent of the knower. Only the self-evident ("It is") is known as what need not be known. An elaborate analysis of self-evidence (II:132-136), "the consciousness that something must be without the consciousness that it is" (i.e., to me), shows that in reflective consciousness it is limited to logical implications (which strictly speaking are not judgments at all). The self-evident content is *known* only accidentally, and so is a *content* only accidentally. This is the element in all that is known which is known as what need not be known, and so satisfies the definition of knowledge. It "demands to be freed from its immanence in the implicational distinction of content and knowing." This is the absolute for knowing (II:136).

The willed content is constituted by willing, but it appears as limiting and foreign to the willing. Reflection does not comprehend, yet demands to comprehend, that this is self-limitation, that the will limits itself to realize itself and so become free. The idealistic view, Kant's, is that the good will is itself the value for which we will to act, that we act objectively in order to be free subjectively. The realistic view is that we act for an objective end. In the case of knowing the realistic view is to be accepted, but in willing the idealistic view, the realistic leading to an infinite regress of means and ends (II:137). *Freedom* of the will is consciousness free from its content, solely constituting its content, making the content a content, creating its distinction from itself. This is the absolute for willing (II:141).

The felt content, not definite in itself, is understood as though it were a unity of content and consciousness, and reflection demands such unity (II:138). Neither the realistic view (value as objective) nor the idealistic view (value as feeling) is preferable; their alternation is stopped only when the unity becomes definite (II:139). In reflection felt content and feeling consciousness are *alternately* distinguished from the value that is their unity; the demand is for them to be *together* distinguished from this unity (II:140). Just as we understand the possibility of known content not being known, and the possibility of willing without the act willed, so, in the appreciation of beauty, we understand the possibility of the self-subsistent unity of felt content and feeling—although these possibilities cannot be realized in reflection, because they involve modes of negation (unrelatedness, negation of the emergent, indifference of being and non-being) unintelligible to the logic of understanding. *Value* is *unity*, that is, indetermination, not identity (II:117), of content and consciousness. This is the absolute for feeling (II:141).

The Absolute is "what is free from the implicational dualism of content and consciousness." There is an[75] absolute for knowing, an absolute for willing, and an absolute for feeling. We cannot say that there are three absolutes or that there is only one; "the absolute is not a known content, about which alone the question 'one or many' has meaning" (II:141). Each is absolute; they are "understood together but not as together" (II:142). The Absolute is either truth or freedom or value, but not all. It is an *alternation* of truth, freedom,[76] and value (II:143).

I will oversimplify still further the subtle and detailed argument[77] of the Presidential Address by restating it in my own words.[78] Philosophy is rational analysis of experience, which is consciousness of some content. There are three conscious functions because there are three ways in which consciousness and content can be related. Content may determine consciousness: this is knowing. Consciousness may determine content: this is willing. Both may determine each other: this is feeling, as in the appreciation of beauty, which is neither purely objective nor purely subjective but a union of the two. Knowing is *truth;* willing is *freedom;* feeling is *value.* Ordinary experience is a confused mixture of the three, but each function can be purged of the accretions of the others and so become pure or absolute. We purge our knowing of its non-cognitive (volitional or emotional) accretions by rejecting its subjective elements[79] (in accordance with Bhattacharyya's law that "consciousness of the false is consciousness of the subjective"). Carried to its theoretic limit, knowing purged of *all* apriori aspects is apprehension of the object as it is in itself; consciousness simply reflects the object. We purge our willing of its non-volitional (cognitive or emotional) accretions by rejecting its objective elements. Willing purged of *all* external aspects is determined entirely from within consciousness, not determined by but completely determining its object. We purge our feeling of its non-emotional (cognitive or volitional) accretions by rejecting the objective or subjective biases which interfere with the aesthetic union of consciousness and content. Feeling purged of *all* abstract[80] (either objective or subjective) aspects is togetherness of subject and object. Knowing freed from all subjectivity is *absolute truth,* uncategorized being in its concrete richness.[81] Willing freed from all objectivity is *absolute freedom,* unrestricted consciousness. Feeling freed from all separateness is *absolute value,* unalloyed bliss. Each is absolute, pure experience, alike negatively as lack of confusion and practically as salvation. But they are incompatible, opposed to each other, incommensurable, neither reducible to each other nor comprehensible under a higher synthesis. They are *alternative absolutes*.

Logic of Alternation

The conclusion is that there are alternative absolutes; more precisely, there are alternative forms of the absolute;[82] still more precisely, the Absolute is an alternation—and even this formula expresses the ineffable doctrine rather awkwardly. Alternation is opposed to condemnation and to integration. According to condemnatory or dogmatic philosophy, there is one Absolute and one path; among opposing views, all but one are false. According to integrative or liberal philosophy, opposing views find ultimate agreement through integration or synthesis; there are many paths leading to the same mountain peak. According to alternative or selective philosophy, there is a choice among incompatible alternatives; there are many paths, each leading to a different mountain peak,[83] and each peak is an absolute summit. The ways to the Absolute diverge; they coincide only at the starting point of ordinary experience where the non-absolutes mingle in confusion. No absolute can judge or be judged by another, for they are incommensurable. There is no external position from which one can be preferred to another, for they are absolute. They cannot be integrated in a higher synthesis, so far as rational philosophy can attain,[84] for they are incompatible. No absolute can claim preference over the others,[85] but each, once accepted, rejects the others. They are true alternatives, and "The Absolute" can only be described as their alternation.[86]

Mention of alternative absolutes sometimes evokes a negative response. This is understandable, in view of the traditional association of absolutism and monism, but its logical ground is questionable. The objection that the Absolute *means* that there is only one can be dismissed as definition by initial predication. The objection that there can be only one absolute Truth shows ignorance of the doctrine; absolute Truth may be one but there are other absolutes besides Truth. The objection that the Absolute should include everything is pantheism; non-dualist Vedanta seeks the Absolute not by including everything but by excluding almost everything. The objection that plural absolutes would limit each other and therefore not be absolute is more serious. This is indeed the point. The theory is that *absolute* Truth, Freedom, and Value, being radically different and incommensurable, do not limit each other. Only *partial* truth, freedom, and value can be associated with and therefore limit each other. Logical questions, however, involve a consideration of the logic of alternation.

A metaphysics is associated with a logic. The logic justifies the metaphysics, but psychologically and existentially the metaphysics determines the logic; "whether one logical system is better than another is settled not by logic but by metaphysic" (II:112).[87] Aristotelian logic is based on *not:* if a judgment is true, its contradictory is not. Dialectical logic is based on *and*, a judgment and its contradictory both accepted: in *anekantavada* (although not as interpreted by Bhattacharyya), the contradictories are true in different respects; in Hegelianism, they are assimilated in a synthesis. The logic of alternation is based on *or*: either alternative may be accepted but not both. The first is the logic of dogmatism (you are wrong); the second is the logic of liberalism (we are both saying the same thing in different ways); the third is the logic of tolerance (this is my way, but I do not deny your right to follow another). The logic of alternation is the logic of choice, commitment, and coexistence. It is the logic of ordinary life, in which we are always making choices, not because only one alternative is correct nor because the alternatives are equivalent but because we must choose and having chosen abide by the choice. It is the logic which justifies alternative forms of the Absolute.

Since[88] there are three conscious functions, there are three alternative forms of the Absolute—absolute knowing, absolute willing, absolute feeling—Truth, Freedom, Value. Different religious or philosophical traditions seek different forms of the Absolute. In "The Concept of Philosophy," his last published work, Bhattacharyya states that the Absolute is understood as Truth in non-dualist Vedanta, as Freedom in "what is loosely called nihilist" Buddhism, and as Value in Hegelianism (II:117). It seemed to me that *value* is not exactly the word for absolute feeling, being rather a generic term for all three (cf. II:137), and that Hegel's intellectual system is not exactly the locus of absolute feeling. In an article "Absolute Feeling"[89] I expressed the opinion that absolute feeling as union of subject and object is *love* in the religious sense of love of God, and that this is the *Christian* ideal; absolute Truth, Freedom, and Love are the goals of Vedanta, Buddhism,[90] and Christianity respectively. It was only after the publication of his collected works that I found that my opinion was substantially in accord with Bhattacharyya's own final opinion. In his last work, *Studies in Yoga Philosophy*, lectures delivered in 1937, four years after the Presidential Address and one year after "The Concept of Philosophy," but not published in his lifetime, he called the absolutes knowledge, will, and *bhakti* (I:305; cf. 289). *Bhakti* means love in the religious sense of love of God. Now, keeping within the context of Hinduism, he assigned the absolutes respectively to Vedanta,[91] Yoga, and Vaishnavism. Vaishnavism is a religion which in its theology and soteriology, and even its Christology and Mariology if these terms can be extended to their Hindu analogues, has much in common with Christianity. But whether we seek the absolutes in non-dualism, Yoga, and Vaishnavism or with a wider perspective in Vedanta, Buddhism, and Christianity, the three religions are *alternative*, incapable of refuting each other and incapable of accepting each other in any synthesis.

The Absolute is ineffable,[92] "an entity that cannot be understood as it is believed, and is speakable only by way of symbolism" (II:116). Perhaps it can be experienced in "suprareflective" consciousness, but it can be understood only negatively as not being what it is not. In neo-Vedanta it is understood as the limit of the process by which experience is purged of the qualifications which make it relative. As there are three such processes, there are three limits, but none can be comprehended by thought or reflection. Absolute Truth, knowing the thing in itself without the subjective categories which give it meaning, can be understood only negatively and spoken only symbolically (II:116). Absolute Freedom, willing without any willed object, is equally meaningless, since what is meant is object. Absolute Love, feeling of subject and object as one though not identical, is the unitive experience of mysticism. The Absolute is incomprehensible, and according to Bhattacharyya it is not one Incomprehensible but three Incomprehensibles.

There are, then, three ways to the Absolute, not converging but diverging. This study will be concluded with a separate discussion of each.[93]

Absolute Knowing

The process of knowing which leads to the Absolute as Truth is analyzed in the article "The Concept of Philosophy,"[94] the last and best known of the works published in his lifetime, which was K. C. Bhattacharyya's contribution to the volume *Contemporary Indian Philosophy*, in which thirteen eminent Indian philosophers stated their philosophical positions.[95] He begins by contrasting his position with Kant's. For Kant the self is a necessity of thought but not knowable. For Bhattacharyya the self is unthinkable but knowable without thinking, "demanding to be known without being thought" (II:107), there being "a *demand*, alternative with other spiritual demands, to realize such knowledge" (II:100). On the critical side he goes beyond contemporary positivists in denying not only metaphysical but even logical *thinking*, since he considers logical forms as mere "shadows of metaphysical symbolisms" and logic a philosophical, not scientific, subject. The extension of thought beyond experience or the possibility of experience is only "the use of the verbal form of thought as a symbol of an unthinkable reality, such symbolizing use not being thinking." On the speculative side, however, he rejects Kantian and positivist agnosticism to assert that the contents of metaphysics are contemplated as true in the faith that only by such contemplation can absolute truth[96] be known (II:101).

Thought[97] or theoretic consciousness is "the understanding of what can be spoken . . . as known or to be known" (II:102). It has four grades: empirical thought, pure objective thought, spiritual thought, transcendental thought. Their contents are respectively fact, self-subsistence, reality, truth. Science deals with fact, which is only contingently speakable, need not be spoken, is *spoken of* as information. Philosophy, which is not a body of judgments but elaboration of the self-evident (II:103), deals with the others, which are intelligible only as spoken, pure thought of a self-evident content not distinguishable from the thought although independent of any individual mind (II:103); it has consequently three grades—philosophy of the object, of the subject, and of truth. Fact is *literally spoken of as meant*; the self-subsistent is *literally spoken* [98] *as meant;* reality is *literally spoken as symbolized;* truth is *spoken symbolically* (II:105).

(1) *Empirical thought,* as Bhattacharyya defines it, is "the theoretic consciousness of a content involving reference to an object that is perceived or imagined to be perceived, such reference being part of the meaning of the content" (II:102). [99] Fact, its content, "is perceivable or has necessary reference to the perceivable, is speakable in the form of a literal judgment and is believed without reference to the speaking of it" (II:107). Only scientific beliefs about fact are "formulable as judgments and literally thinkable" (II:106); in this the positivists are right. But science does not recognize any mystery, or any sacredness, in its perceived or imagined objects. For science the object is intrinsically knowable; there is nothing in the object to *make* it known; it is just what is known or at least knowable (II:108). It is not only knowable but also usable, and it is this "wrong spiritual attitude of science toward the object," not any inadequacy in scientific theory, which provokes a philosophy which goes beyond science, based on the spiritual demand "that nature should be contemplated and not merely used" (II:108).

(2) *Pure objective* (or contemplative) *thought* is thought of objective but imperceptible contents (II:102), that is, universals. The self-subsistent object "has no necessary reference to the perceivable," [100] but "has necessary reference to the speaking of it" (II:110), is "believed only as it is spoken" (II:107), is constituted by being spoken (II:112)—a conceptual theory of universals, which makes them independent of particulars but dependent on the thinking (although not literally thinking) process, although Bhattacharyya calls it *realism* in contrast with the "solipsistic idealism" of science (II:108). Anything speakable "is understood in necessary reference either to sense-perception or to the speaking of it," and the latter, not restricted by perception, is believed as independent of the belief of any individual mind and so self-evident. The self-evident understood in the objective attitude is the self-subsistent object. It may be inaccessible to the mind, and so is of no interest to science, which is concerned only with intrinsically knowable objects. The philosophy (not science) of the self-subsistent object comprises logic, which studies the form of the object, and metaphysics, which studies the object itself (II:110). Logic, a system of "speech-created forms of mean-

ing" (II:112), presupposes metaphysics (II:111), which "defines itself in logic" (II:113), and insofar as there are alternative metaphysics there are also alternative logics (II:112). No metaphysical concept, however, is intelligible without reference to the "subject or spirit" which goes beyond metaphysics (II:111). Alleged deductive proof in metaphysics is a sham. Metaphysical abstractions (considered high-grade abstractions by metaphysicians and diseases of speech by positivists) are "symbolic meanings which derive their whole value for belief from the spiritual experiences that they symbolise" (II:112). Pure objective thought, therefore, necessarily leads to spiritual thought. And it is the contrast between logic, the entities of which are obviously not real, and metaphysics, where they are supposed to be real, which suggests the distinction between the self-subsistent and the real. This distinction is verified in the consciousness of objectivity as a symbol of the real subject (II:113).

(3) *Spiritual* (or enjoying) *thought* is introspection, theoretic consciousness which rejects the objective attitude, the enjoying understanding of a content "as symbolised by an objectively contemplated meaning" (II:113). It is not mere consciousness of reality but is reality (II:114). Its content is neither the interior of the body (which is fact) nor the mental (which is self-subsistent object) but *I*, spoken as though it were an object but understood as what object is not, as the speaking subjectivity (II:113). Spiritual (unlike psychological) introspection involves the explicit consciousness of *being* what is spoken—*I*. The subject, however, is not enjoyed alone. Something else is always enjoyed along with, and in reference to, the subject. There may be consciousness of the subject as embodied, or consciousness of personal relation to other selves, or consciousness of the over-personal self related to *I* by identity in difference—a relation unintelligible in the objective attitude (II:114). This religious experience is not of *I* as symbolized by something but of the over-personal reality as symbolized by *I*. Symbolizing by *I* is a non-theoretic experience of self-negation, not consciousness of yourself as nothing but consciously being nothing. "What emerges to *theoretic* religious consciousness" is the over-personal reality alone, "the enjoyed fulness of being" which transcends both objectivity and subjectivity (II:115).

Taking a dialectical glance downward at this point of the ascent, Bhattacharyya notes that individual religious experiences are different, not to be systematized by secular reason, but presenting themselves in alternative systems. Each generates its own philosophy of religion, metaphysics, and logic (differences in logical theory being ultimately religious differences). Philosophy is systematic symbolism, which necessarily admits of *alternatives*, so "there is no question of philosophy progressing towards a single unanimously acceptable solution" (II:115).

(4) *Transcendental thought* has for its content neither fact (things) nor self-subsistent object (universals) nor reality (individual self) but absolute Truth. In the spiritual thought of religion the subject negates itself enjoyingly, not theoretically, but this involves theoretic consciousness of the possibility of the individual self's being unreal. "The denial of the *I* is possible because we already believe that the absolute is" (II:115). The Absolute, not to be confused with the over-personal reality, is meant negatively as what the subject *I* is not, understood negatively but believed positively. Whereas the over-personal reality is symbolized as *I* and expressed literally as a self, Truth is symbolized as *not-I* and so not reality, not to be enjoyed, and not literally expressible at all. Unlike literally speakable reality, which is revealed by being spoken, Truth, "being spoken as what the speaking *I* is not," is self-revealing (II:116). Far from being identical with the Self, as classical non-dualism teaches, *Brahman* or absolute Truth is definable as what Self is not.

To be spoken at all, even symbolically, an entity must be somehow distinct, and so distinguished from something, but the Absolute has nothing outside itself from which to be distinguished. It can be distinguished only from alternative forms of itself. Truth is the Absolute, but the Absolute is not necessarily Truth. It may be Truth, or it may be what Truth is not, or it may be their indeterminate togetherness—absolute Truth, Freedom, or Value (II:116). The theory of alternative forms of the Absolute is not a paradoxical accretion to the theory of the Absolute but is what makes possible any *theory* of the Absolute at all.

Absolute Willing

The process of willing which leads to the Absolute as Freedom has its fullest systematic presentation in the book *The Subject as*

Freedom already analyzed. This book, however, was written before Bhattacharyya had formulated the doctrine of the alternative forms of the Absolute. Knowing and willing are not clearly distinguished, and absolute Subject as absolute Freedom seems to be also absolute Truth. Still, if read with care, the book is not inconsistent with the later doctrine, which may even be said to be implicit in it. His final doctrine might be formulated: *the Subject as Freedom, the Object*[101] *as Truth, their Unity*[102] *as Love.* In *The Subject as Freedom* the dialectic is rigorous pursuit of the subjective attitude. In "The Concept of Philosophy" it is rather different: the first step is from perceivable fact to self-subsistent object; the second step is from objectivity to subjectivity; the third step is from subjectivity to Truth. The individual subject or self known in introspection is the antepenultimate stage in the former work, the penultimate in the latter. In the former this is transcended in favor of the larger, non-individual, subject, the greater *I*, and this in turn in favor of Freedom itself as what subjectivity is. In the latter it is transcended in favor of Truth, the absolute object, more fundamental than facts or universals but opposed to the subject, defined indeed as what the subject *I* is not. The two concepts of the Absolute are not only different but opposed. In the article absolute Truth is *Being*: "the absolute as transcending the enjoyed reality of religion is positive being (truth) or positive non-being (freedom) or their positive indetermination (value)" (II:117). And in the last sentence of the book freedom is opposed to being: "freedom without being" (I:92).[103] The *subjective attitude* leads to the subject as Freedom. *Theoretic consciousness* leads to the non-subject as Truth.

K. C. Bhattacharyya's last and longest works, not published in his lifetime, are two series of lectures, on Sankhya and Yoga,[104] delivered at the Indian Institute of Philosophy at Amalner in 1937. These ancient systems are treated with the same originality which characterized his earlier studies of Vedanta, Jainism, and Kant (I:xi). In Sankhya especially, where the classical commentators "do not help us much" but the sources "are suggestive enough to tempt us to construct the system anew," the reconstruction "involves supplying of missing links from one's imagination," without which "one cannot be said to understand Sankhya as a philosophy" (I:127). In both studies technical terms are given in Sanskrit, a source of difficulty for the non-Sanskritist reader. But the ancient traditions are presented as living philosophies.[105] The *Studies in Sankhya* are of great intrinsic interest, with more metaphysical detail than any of his other works. There are some characteristic Bhattacharyya expressions. *Prakriti* or matter, traditionally described as constituted by the *gunas* or qualities as a rope by its strands, is said to be not a unity or substratum or togetherness of the *gunas* but their *alternation* (I:200). The doctrine of alternative absolutes is discussed: "knowing, willing, and feeling amount to self-becoming in the region of the absolute" (I:181); "the aesthetic (*tanmatra*) in fact is an absolute mentality like willing (*ahamkara*) and certitude (*buddhi*)" (I:180). He even suggests what seems like the beginning of a further development if not radical revision of this doctrine when he says, "These forms of the absolute mind are really three stages: *buddhi* as self-knowing becomes *ahamkara* as self-willing which in its turn becomes *tanmatra* as self-feeling" (I:181). Were this sentence elaborated in an article, it might be considered a fourth phase (hierarchical absolutes) in the development of Bhattacharyya's philosophical thought, but by itself it is only a suggestion of what a fourth phase might have been. Sankhya dualism also suggests the simultaneous attainment of alternative absolutes: the consummation of knowing, which is the "reversion" of willing, is not "eternal quiescent knowledge," which would be the self, but mind distinguishing, defining, or detaching itself from the self to be lost in unmanifest matter, while the self is left "in its eternally manifest solitariness" (I:144)—which seems to mean mind absolutely knowing the thing-in-itself and self absolutely willing without any object. In general, however, this work is of relatively little relevance to the present study, since Sankhya, with its interest in the world, is not like Vedanta and Yoga exclusively concerned with the search for the Absolute. *Studies in Yoga*, on the other hand, are concerned with the dialectic of will.

Knowing is passive, but willing is active. Non-dualist Vedanta is the way of knowing: its steps are the rejection of illusions; its goal is not to do anything but to know. Yoga is the way of doing: its steps are forms of behavior; its goal is not to know anything but to will. "All spiritual *activity* is yoga" (I:286), which understands freedom conatively (I:253); willing, for Yoga, is self-conscious subjectivity (I:221). Its positive downward trend is toward *bhoga* (egoistic activity). Its negative upward trend is willing to abstain from egoistic willing, willing to approach and attain *samadhi* (I:224), *inward* willing (I:284). The practice of yoga is spiritual willing, conditioned by knowledge, in the discipline leading to absolute Freedom. It involves knowledge only contingently (I:225); in it both knowing and feeling are "implicit willing" (I:283). Yoga is "spiritual willing for the free being or active quiescence of the spirit" (I:225),[106] the "essential or spiritual form of willing" (I:284). The activity toward *samadhi* is free willing; *samadhi* itself is free being.[107] Yoga as free willing for free being is the conscious activity of the mind to overcome its differentiation into states. The "will to be in the knowing attitude for freedom from knowledge" is the will to contemplate the mystery of the absolute Freedom through which free will itself emerges, the "freedom to create freedom," which is God (I:227).

The realizing of freedom, taken as a knowing process in Vedanta and Sankhya and a feeling process in Vaishnavism, is for Yoga literal willing (I:285). Freedom as a mental state is psychologically intelligible only as freedom of the will, and this is yoga (I:287). Yoga philosophy reduces the mystical consciousness of spiritual activity to a *practical* psychology (I:286). Freedom is first known as freedom from evil (I:284), but it is not necessary to begin at the lowest step (I:306). The first two steps constitute the ethical and religious setting of the yoga activity (I:309); the next three are the process of energizing the body as an organ of the spirit; the last three are purely spiritual willing (I:311).[108] In religion freedom from the body may come through grace, but in yoga it must be achieved by the will. The outgoing assertive bodily willing is replaced by ingoing retractive bodily willing leading to tranquil posture, equitable vital flow, and the reversal of sense activity (I:289, 312).

Samadhi, the goal of Yoga, is not *knowing* but "freedom beyond knowledge" (I:304). Conscious awareness of self as free from mind, which is realized by God, is only faith for man (I:322). God is a postulate, not an object, of the yogi's spiritual realization (I:318).[109] He is not known or intuited in *samadhi* (I:320); he is silent, abstaining from revealing himself, as in *pralaya*, the divine sleep where all things cease (I:324). Neither is *samadhi feeling*

(I:297). *Samadhi* is the culmination of *willing*, or rather an *alternation* of willing and not-willing, where the willing is the negative willing of withdrawal and not-willing is contemplation[110] of the mystery of absolute Freedom or God (I:227). Yoga realizes freedom of the will as an end or good achieved by right, not as an imperative obeyed by grace, and so is nowise religious but supersedes religion (I:288). It also supersedes ethics, beyond good and evil (I:305).[111] Relapse from superconscious freedom to knowledge of mind as distinct from self has its full maturation in "the four-fold knowledge of evil, cause of evil, freedom from evil, and means to freedom" (I:304).[112] But in the supreme *samadhi*, where the identity of self and mind is taken not as mind but as self (I:296), reality emerges as the "mystery of absolute freedom" (I:324), where *samadhi* can only be described as "the activity of changeless self-reproduction" (I:225, 258). This is absolute activity, will, freedom, or subject—the opposite of passivity, knowledge, truth, or object.

Freedom in the sense of indeterminism is considered in the paper (date unknown) "Reality of the Future." The future is contingent and undetermined, not what will be but what can be, inferred as what will be if nothing interferes (II:273). It is real to us in two ways—by will and by faith, which are antithetical attitudes (II:274). Faith can be reduced to ideal willing, or will to faith that "my will is coming," but neither reduction is justified (II:277). When the objective means seem unpredictable, faith lets us believe that the end will come nevertheless. But if will does not give place to faith, it may persist as a demonic *(asurika)* aspiration to make history by exploiting objects as means, as in hypnotism (II:278). Will and faith are alternative attitudes toward the undetermined, and their dualism cannot be overcome (II:274).

Absolute Feeling

The process of feeling which leads to the Absolute as Value is discussed in two essays, "Artistic Enjoyment" and "The Beautiful and the Ugly," written in 1925 and published together in *Studies in Philosophy* under the title "The Concept of *Rasa.*" *Rasa* (flavor) means either aesthetic enjoyment or that which is aesthetically enjoyed (I:349). The first of the two essays develops the dialectic of feeling on four levels.

(1) *Primary feeling* is direct feeling of an object, enjoying it. The contrast of subject and object characteristic of knowing and willing is obscured. The subject affects the object and is affected by it. The object appears not as mere fact but as having a value, while the subject feels attracted into the object rather than detached from it (I:350). This confused unity has alternative directions: in the objective, self-feeling lapses and object alone is perceived with its value; in the subjective, object becomes indefinite while subject retains its feeling attitude (I:355) and absorbs the object (I:356).

(2) *Sympathetic feeling* is feeling of feeling. Its object is another person's feeling. Sympathy is not a duplicate of the other person's feeling. In sympathizing with a child enjoying his toy I am not interested in the toy but in his enjoyment. "Sympathy with joy is also joy but it is freer than the primary joy." I do not lose the sense of distinction between my feeling and the child's as he loses the distinction between his feeling and its object (I:350).[113] Sympathy also has alternative forms: in projective sympathy, I feel out toward the other person; in assimilative sympathy, I draw him into myself (I:356).

(3) *Contemplative feeling* is sympathy with sympathy. Three persons are involved. When I enjoy contemplating an old man watching his grandchild playing with a toy, the child's joy in the toy, the grandfather's sympathetic joy, and my contemplative joy are on different levels. I am interested in the child's feeling reflected in the grandfather's as an eternal emotion or value. I no longer feel the distinction between my feeling and the child's; I become impersonal (I:353). The expression of the object is detached from the particularity of fact as an eternal value. Beauty is such an eternal value, seen not as a quality of the object or another object beside it but as the reality to which the object itself is somehow adjectival (I:352). All feeling involves identification of subject and object, but in contemplative feeling both identity and difference are explicit. Subject merges into object and object is dissolved in subject (I:359).

(4) *Artistic enjoyment* is sympathy with sympathy when one or both of the persons sympathized with is imaginary (I:353). Feeling depicted in art is contemplated as sympathized with by the Heart Universal, the felt person in general, in which the person contemplating the feeling merges his personal heart. In the en-

joyment of the beauty of a natural object, the third person, who feels the object, is someone in general (I:354). The beauty of an object involves expression, detachment from the object, and eternity—projections respectively of primary, sympathetic, and contemplative feeling; though the feelings of the three persons may be different emotional levels in the same individual (I:355). Artistic enjoyment has alternative directions. In the projective or dynamically creative direction, the feeling becomes objective yet without getting entangled in fact, transfiguring fact into value —freedom in spite of enjoying contact. In the assimilative, abstractive, or contemplative direction, the feeling is subjective detachment in which the value of the object is abstracted and reposefully enjoyed—enjoyment of reality in spite of detachment (I:357). In either case the enjoyer identifies himself with the eternal value (I:356). This artistic or aesthetic enjoyment is the highest feeling, realization of eternal value, "identification with the aesthetic essence without loss of freedom" (I:355).

Non-Indians, generally impressed by the beauty and refinement of Indian art, are sometimes perplexed by the striking ugliness of some works, even representations of deity. The aesthetic value of ugliness is discussed in the essay "The Beautiful and the Ugly." Beauty is objective: "the aesthetic attitude does not create but only discovers beauty or ugliness" (I:358). It is also subjective: "what particular symmetrical form is beautiful depends on the intuition of the artist." In Indian art, which "is prevailingly abstractive or contemplative in character and not dynamically creative," the aesthetic essence is conceived as a subjective absolute or *rasa* rather than an objective absolute or beauty (I:357).[114] Even when discovered, the aesthetic quality is discovered not by cognition but by feeling, which implies identification of subject and object (I:358). But their distinction is also felt—not at all in primary feeling, explicitly in sympathetic feeling, merged with identity in contemplative feeling. Where enjoyment, the feeling of identity, is subordinate to pain, the feeling of difference, a feeling of ugliness emerges (I:359). It is a power, not necessarily actualized, of the artistic spirit to transmute painful feelings into enjoyment (I:360). *Aesthetic effort* deepens the feeling of ugliness into enjoyment and so realizes the ugly, in the perspective of its infinite setting, as beautiful (I:362). The emergence of Beauty from the ugly, Bhattacharyya remarks, does credit both to Indian art itself and to its theory (I:363).

Value, the content of feeling, is analyzed in the article "The Concept of Value" published in 1934. The analysis reflects the influence, but nowise a mere following, of Kant:[115] "the feeling that I reflectively feel is not taken as any one's feeling in particular: it is unappropriated or impersonalised rather than universalised" (II:287). Unlike known object, which is completely distinct from the knowing, felt value is only imperfectly distinct from the feeling (II:285) and cannot be spoken without reference to the feeling. The value is identified with the object, although the object is not identified with the value. Speaking of a value in an object indicates the objectivity of value resulting from the impersonalization of the feeling (II:288). Value is objective, independent of valuation (II:290); the object *is* beautiful, not merely to me (II:287). But it is not an adjective of the object (II:289)—although by a necessary illusion it is spoken of as if it were. Expression of felt character (It is a cool breeze) leads to expression of feeling (How cool is the breeze!) and this in turn to expression of feeling of feeling (How I enjoy the cool breeze!). In *feeling of feeling* the value is completely freed from the object and becomes absolute (II:291).

Coordinate with the value of a known content is that of a willed content (II:285). Willing as such is not value (II:293); to say, "We should act thus," is only an imperative. But to exclaim,*"How* we should act thus!" is to *feel* the sacredness of the ought (II:292). Sacredness is the holiness of an impersonal will felt to be embodied in the object, as beauty is an impersonal joy embodied in it (II:293). The value of an act depends on the moral value of the ideal impersonal willing which determines it, and the judgment on it is aesthetic relative to the judgment on that ideal willing (II:294). What is eternally willed is goodness or freedom (II:295), which is *felt* "as negation of the objectivity of the subject and yet as its constitutive reality" (II:297). Feeling or valuation is thus a process intermediate between knowing and willing (II:298).

This distinction between value of a known object and value of a willed act suggests an answer to the question raised above whether absolute feeling should not be called Love rather than Value. The content of feeling in general is value, but it has alternative modes. The value of known object is beauty; that of willed act is love. We might say that love is the subjective, beauty the objective, aspect of that value which is felt by union of subject and object, and that absolute Value is an alternation of absolute Beauty and absolute Love.[116]

Conclusion

A fourth phase of K. C. Bhattacharyya's thought is constituted by speculations between his final retirement in 1937 and his death in 1949. With failing eyesight but unfailing mind, he developed especially the abstract logical aspect of the dialectic of alternation. These speculations survive, probably not permanently, in a mass of written fragments, never edited (I:x), and in the recollections, never reduced to writing, of conversations with his sons Gopinath, the editor of his works, and Kalidas, whose sympathy with his father's philosophical thought makes him his intellectual heir.[117] Philosophical reflection, he said, begins with the existence of what is given in experience. By logic we discover interpretations of the given recognized as possibilities, and from these other possibilities are derived. In the realm of possibility, which is the domain of logic, there is no affirmation. The basic logical category is negation, including double, triple, and quadruple negation, by which novel possibilities are developed, equally possible but incompatible. Any possibility may become actual, but conflict among actuals is resolved by recognizing them as alternatively actual. Possibility and actuality are themselves alternative attitudes. Underlying such dialectic is the linguistic analysis of the common structure of all possibilities, a study which analyzes the "mere forms" of semantic thought and the "pure forms" of syntactic thought. Both the logical and the linguistic analyses were elaborated in an involved dialectic, but neither was systematized.

Neo-Vedanta search for the Absolute is continued in Kalidas Bhattacharyya's book *Alternative Standpoints in Philosophy*,[118] the lucid style of which is a refreshing contrast to that of his father's works. His philosophical thought is a continuation of his father's philosophy, but it is developed in an original way, and his epistemological subjectivism is opposed to his father's realism. The logic of alternation provides the structure of his thought. When one alternative is asserted as actual, the other alternatives are rejected or ignored or subordinated or included, and by the dialectic resulting from these processes the chosen alternative is developed to its logical conclusion. The central problem of philosophy, he says, is how knowledge of object is possible, since knowledge, the subjective feeling of an object, and object, known as not itself knowledge, are so opposed in nature that their conjunction seems contradictory. Alternative attitudes offer alternative solutions. A philosopher does not become an idealist or realist through arguments, but "at the very start, according as he begins with the subjective or the objective attitude; he only interprets phenomena from the standpoint he has already assumed."[119] If we assume the *subjective attitude*, we have *knowing*, in which the subject determines or creates its object. If we assume the *objective attitude*, we have *feeling*, in which the object is felt with immediate certainty. If we assume the *dialectical attitude*, we have *willing* in which a dialectical synthesis of subject and object is attained. In the first case knowing *subordinates* feeling; in the second feeling *rejects* knowing; in the third willing while subjective *incorporates* the objective. The alternative philosophies are equally correct but incompatible. Knowing, feeling, and willing tolerate each other in practical life, but in reflection each demands to be absolute—pure subjectivity as absolute knowing or Truth, pure object as absolute feeling or Beauty, dialectical synthesis as absolute willing or Goodness. The ultimate problem of philosophy is the status of alternation itself. For Buddhism there is no reality but only alternative philosophies; for Jainism reality itself is alternative; for Vedanta there is one reality but alternative standpoints from which it can be viewed. The alternation of these alternative theories of alternation is the last word of the philosophy of alternative standpoints.

While Kalidas Bhattacharyya's administrative duties as chairman, dean, and vice-chancellor at Visvabharati University have interfered with his philosophical publication, his recent philosophical speculation has involved further development of the concept of alternation. Besides the alternation of knowing, feeling, and willing, he says,[120] there is a cross alternation in which each may be alternatively considered in terms of either of the others. Besides pure knowing, which is purely subjective, there is knowing of objects, which is knowing in terms of feeling. Besides pure feeling, which is purely objective, there is feeling of self, which is feeling in terms of knowing. The concept of coincidence must be joined to that of alternation: the line dividing adjacent squares belongs alternatively and entirely to either because the squares coincide on one side. Alternatives diverge, but there is a sense in which they converge also.

The neo-Vedanta of K. C. Bhattacharyya and his son, based on the tradition of non-dualist Vedanta, strongly influenced by German idealism, having its literary expression in English, is a philosophy of universal appeal independent of any cultural context. Like classical Vedanta it is not a theory or system but a way of thinking capable of indefinite development and application. Its most significant features are the logical method of alternation and the metaphysical doctrine of alternative absolutes.

Logically alternation is exclusive disjunction (p or q but not both). Contemporary symbolic logic is usually developed in terms of negation (not p), conjunction (p and q), and inclusive disjunction (p or q or both); exclusive disjunction plays a minor role in the abstract systematization. In life, however, it plays a major role. Such questions as "Tea or coffee?" "Shall I marry Tom or Dick?" are not ordinarily answered by "both." Life consists largely of situations in which exclusive alternatives are presented for choice. All are possible; one is to be actual. The problems may be trivial, as which stairs shall I go up. They may be important, involving an irrevocable choice of spouse, vocation, or religion. They may not be simple; when one potentiality is actualized, the others may be rejected or ignored or subordinated or included, depending on the whole situation. It is by choice among exclusive alternatives that we conduct our lives and make ourselves what we become. But alternation, so obviously important in practice, is also important in theory. Even in so abstract a realm as that of mathematics an equation may have alternative roots. In concrete reality alternation is commonplace, not only because the contingent truth is dependent on determining factors but also because, besides truth, other values, moral and aesthetic, are also possible. The neo-Vedanta logic of alternation is an attempt to systematize abstractly the structure of valid thought which is applicable to concrete reality.

Metaphysically the doctrine of alternative absolutes or alternative forms of the Absolute or the Absolute as Alternation is an original approach to the perennial central problem of philosophy. On the one hand, it avoids the pluralism or relativism which results from abandoning this problem as insoluble. On the other hand, it avoids the monism or abstractionism which results from a too facile solution. Based on the psychological distinction of the knowing, willing, and feeling functions of the Self and the epistemological distinction of objective, subjective, and dialectical attitudes correlated with them (although how correlated remains controversial), this doctrine dares to contemplate even the Absolute in terms of exclusive disjunction. Practically, its applications are beneficent. In religion and in politics[121] it supports, as against either dogmatism or liberalism, a policy of coexistence which tolerates alternative principles without compromising one's own. Theoretically, one form of the Absolute is distinguished from another but nowise relative to the other. The Absolute, first recognized as the Indefinite underlying the manifold of definite objects, then as the Subject with which the Indefinite is identified, finally as the Alternation emerging from the Subject's incompatible functions, is spoken (alternatively contemplated, asserted, or enjoyed) in a symbol which refuses to deny the richness of its meaning by claiming a transcendent consistency beyond the actual consistency of each form. The Self finds its absoluteness in alternative ways—by denying itself, by denying the not-self, or by denying their separation. The Absolute is Truth, or Freedom, or Love, and the important word is *or*.

Neo-Vedanta, a fruit of the Indian philosophical renaissance of the twentieth century, is a mature philosophy. The youthful philosophical enthusiasm which pursues the metaphysical will-o'-the-wisp of an Absolute which has everything issues too often in an uncritical satisfaction that this has been attained or an overcritical rejection of metaphysics as futile. Neo-Vedanta is existentially oriented but phenomenologically grounded in experience. It seeks the Absolute not through a monistic category of understanding but through an analysis of the cognitive, conative, and emotional aspects of experience, and it recognizes that this can be done in different ways. As a way of thinking its accomplishments are impressive and its possibilities unlimited. "In a great and tangled movement of men and their ideas, the world is making itself over . . . and we have to reach for ideas big enough to grasp the magnitude of what is taking place."[122] The Absolute as Alternation is an idea at once profound and comprehensive, and peculiarly relevant in a world which is many in concerns and ideologies but one in a no longer divisible destiny.

NOTES

1. I am indebted to the Trustees of Tufts College for the sabbatical leave of absence, to the Rockefeller Foundation for the financial grant, to Visvabharati University for the hospitality, and to Professor (now Vice-Chancellor) Kalidas Bhattacharyya for the instruction which made possible the study on which this article is based.

2. Vedanta epistemologists also recognize three other sources of knowledge—analogy, assumption, and negation. K. C. Bhattacharyya analyzes the six ways of knowing in his *Studies in Vedantism* (I:71-90). [References in the Introduction are to *Studies in Philosophy*, volumes I and II, a collection of K. C. Bhattacharyya's philosophical works. The three articles by K. C. Bhattacharyya reprinted in this book are from volume II of that collection. For the convenience of readers, the following corresponding page numbers of reprinted article to *Studies in Philosophy*, volume II, are presented: "Place of the Indefinite in Logic" (II:225-239); "The Subject as Freedom" (II:19-92); "The Concept of the Absolute and Its Alternative Forms" (II:125-143).]

3. For brief studies of some other neo-Vedanta philosophers see my article "Contemporary Vedanta Philosophy," *Review of Metaphysics* 9(1955-1956):485-504, 662-680; 10(1956-1957):122-157.

4. His life was spent in a succession of minor teaching and administrative posts in the Bengal Educational Service, and it was only after retirement that he attained the prestige of the King George V chair. His students say that he always considered their philosophical suggestions sympathetically, often adding his own arguments to support them, thus making the students feel elated, but then proceeded to criticize them. Meanwhile he supported a large joint family on his meager salary. He was known for austerity of life, geniality of personality, and integrity of character, and was interested in literature, music, and the struggle for independence. For a biographical sketch by his nephew Professor P. J. Chaudhury of Presidency College, Calcutta, see *Krishna Chandra Bhattacharyya Memorial Volume* (Amalner: Indian Institute of Philosophy, 1958), pp. i-viii.

5. His originality, says D. M. Datta, "lies in his compact, irresistible logical chain of arguments."

6. The most extended study is by D. M. Datta, *The Chief Currents of Contemporary Philosophy* (Calcutta: Calcutta University Press, 1950), pp. 126-145. Other studies have been based on single works, *The Subject as Freedom*: D. M. Datta, "Two Indian Philosophers," *Aryan Path* 6(1935):394-398; K. K. Bagchi, "Notion of Epistemology in K. C. Bhattacharyya," *Philosophical Quarterly* 36(1963):93-99; G. B. Burch, "The Neo-Vedanta of K. C. Bhattacharyya," *International Philosophical Quarterly* 5(1965):304-310; or "The Concept of Philosophy": P. T. Raju, *Idealistic Thought of India* (Cambridge: Harvard University Press, 1953), pp. 354-375; R. Das, "Acharya Krishnachandra's Conception of

Philosophy," *Journal of the Indian Academy of Philosophy* 2(1963):1-13; or else on conversations: G. B. Burch, "Contemporary Vedanta Philosophy," *Review of Metaphysics* 9(1955-1956):485-496.

7. "There remains over an immense mass of manuscripts which will, perhaps, remain unpublished for all time to come" (I:v).

8. His oral teaching, on the other hand, was a model of clarity, fluency, and persuasiveness. He could write clearly if he chose, as is shown by the clear and graceful style of his "Svaraj in Ideas," *Visvabharati Quarterly* 20(1954):103-114; reprinted in Silver Jubilee Issue, 25(1960):295-303. An earlier paper, "Fifty Years of British Education," is said to have the same clear style.

9. A proposal in 1942 by Gopinath Bhattacharyya that his father clarify his writings orally in order that Gopinath might compose a commentary on them was abandoned when they calculated that at the rate they were going it would take fifty years.

10. When told D. M. Datta was writing a section on him for his *Contemporary Philosophy*, he said he did not realize he had any system of philosophy.

11. The first and second together correspond to the "first phase" in my discussion in "Contemporary Vedanta Philosophy."

12. *Brihadaranyaka Upanishad*, 2:3:6, 3:9:26, 4:2:4, 4:4:22, 4:5:15.

13. Awarded to young scholars of the highest distinction, on the basis of examinations and written work, with the expectation of a thesis of outstanding merit.

14. Appearance of these words in contemporary Indian philosophical works is usually a sign of his influence.

15. Here and elsewhere I have italicized at discretion.

16. In discussing Yoga he says: "The given-ness of the object in ordinary perception is not an ultimate inexplicability as it is to Kant but implies the consciousness that I have to know it better and the object has to reveal itself more frankly" (I:293).

17. I am indebted to Mrs. James H. Woods for the suggestion that I systematically substitute the synonym *affirmation* for Bhattacharyya's word *position*.

18. I mean *difficult* literally, not ironically, not suggesting that it is fallacious.

19. This system of logic is further developed by an elaborate theory of relations in the paper "The Definition of Relation as a Category of Existence" (written 1918, published posthumously, II:245-257).

20. Neo-Vedanta offers no rational refutation of positivism. "Beliefs in science alone are formulable as judgments and literally thinkable" (II:106).

21. *Chandogya Upanishad*, 6:8-16.

22. The first edition of this book, which is suitable for reading in graduate or undergraduate courses on metaphysics, is obtainable from the publisher (Indian Institute of Philosophy, Amalner, Jalgaon).

23. "Widely different from how it has been understood by English-

speaking peoples," but "amply supported by German and Continental commentaries," says Kalidas Bhattacharyya (*Memorial Volume*, p. 227)—but he remarked to me that his father was always "going beyond," i.e., correcting, Kant. (The editor includes this among the original works in volume II, not among the critical historical studies in volume I.)

24. Cf.: "Perceived object necessarily refers to the body and implies distinction from it but the body does not imply distinction from the object but implies only distinction from I" (*Studies in Sankhya*, I:159). The external world is the projection as phenomenon, through the necessity of experience, of the self as identified with the body (I:160).

25. Compare the assertion symbol of *Principia Mathematica*.

26. This interpretation of the article, for which I am indebted to Kalidas Bhattacharyya, may "go beyond" the text a little (representing, as he said, his own rather than his father's philosophy).

27. I say framework, not foundation. He says elsewhere (II:115) that logic is based on metaphysics.

28. *Philosophical Quarterly* 7(1932):387-396.

29. *Ibid.*, pp. 397-404.

30. Note that he does not restrict the terms *true* and *false* to propositions.

31. This way of putting it is in the spirit of Jain logic, which however is not mentioned in this article.

32. "I believed in a content which was [!] not fact nor absolute nought" (II:190). I do not quite understand this, in view of the definition, reaffirmed in this article (II:186), of fact as what is believed.

33. He also considers it the basic principle of the Madhyamika Buddhist philosophy of Nagarjuna (*The Central Philosophy of Buddhism*[London: George Allen & Unwin, 1955], p. 209).

34. "Speakable," capable of being expressed at all—a category more inclusive than "intelligible."

35. Faith seeking understanding is perhaps the best approach to this article, which is hard to understand unless its truth is presupposed.

36. This sentence, which is indeed "paradoxical, if not obviously false," seems to be the crux of the argument.

37. Even the "primal certitude" *I am I* really means *mind is not I*, a negative judgment (I:184).

38. The chronological order of publication does not follow the logical development of ideas, as three of the four preliminary articles (1928, 1931, 1931, 1932) were published after the book (1930). But we may reasonably suppose that Bhattacharyya, never one to rush into print, had the substance of the articles clearly in mind, and very likely reduced to writing, before delivering the lectures which became the book.

39. By Kalidas Bhattacharyya (*Memorial Volume*, p. 220; cf. II:3).

40. With serious shortcomings: a persisting objective attitude in the first critique, admission of the unknowable reality ("an unwarrantable surrender to realism"), denial of self-knowledge, disbelief in the possibility of a spiritual discipline of the theoretic reason through which

self-knowledge may be attainable, confusion of undeniability with truth (II:31).

41. This is the way of knowledge *(jnana-marga)* of traditional non-dualist Vedanta, opposed to the way of morality *(karma-marga)* involved in the "good life."

42. The thirty-two paragraphs of chapter 2 are devoted to the definition of this concept.

43. But like spatiality, studied independently of any object in geometry, Kalidas Bhattacharyya remarked.

44. The *maya* and *moksha* of traditional Vedanta.

45. Hegelianism, coordinate dualism of psychic and object, psychic as comprehending object as a real element, experience-unity of subject and object, and distinction between enjoying and contemplative modes of knowing are also criticized and rejected.

46. "The objectivity of other perceived objects is constituted by their position relative to the percipient's body" (II:4-50) , hence the latter, which has no perceived position (II:63) , involves "the mystic awareness of dissociation from the object in which subjectivity consists" (II:51).

47. "To those who would not go farther in psychology [i.e., behaviorists] , introspection is only observation of the indefinite body-interior" (II:62).

48. The asymmetry of *distinction* is a dialectical principle found throughout Bhattacharyya's works.

49. The thirteen paragraphs of chapter 4 are devoted to the analysis of this concept.

50. Fact in general means what is asserted, but the meaning of fact-hood as a predicate apart from the assertion changes as we pass from perceived object to perceived body, felt body, absence, and image.

51. *Sought*, in this context, seems to indicate the object-directed constructive faculty *(maya)*, whereas *demanding* indicates the subject-oriented self-realizing activity *(moksha)*.

52. The *Atman* of traditional Vedanta, contrasted with the individual self *jiva.*

53. The whole scheme is summarized in the last chapter, which may therefore be read as a summary of the book—but a *sutra*-like summary intelligible only as a reminder of what has already been studied in detail.

54. The dialectic may be summarized in eleven steps: environment, perceived body, felt body, absence, image, idea, thought, feeling, introspection, non-individual self, freedom.

55. *Intelligibility and the Philosophy of Nothingness*, trans. R. Schinzinger (Tokyo: Maruzen, 1958), p. 129.

56. *L'Evolution Créatrice* (Paris: Presses Universitaires, 1962), p. 270.

57. These words are used in a way the opposite of what one might expect: "as knowledge deepens, there is a *regress* to prior presuppositions, the felt body etc., up to feeling" (II:75).

58. The influence of Jain logic on K. C. Bhattacharyya's philosophy (my sabbatical project) was the point of departure for this study. For Jain

logic, see my article "Seven-Valued Logic in Jain Philosophy," *International Philosophical Quarterly* 4(1964):68-93.

59. *Prameya* knowable, *kamala* lotus, *martanda* sun: "the light which makes the truth unfold." *Prameyakamal Martand* by Shri Prabha Chandra (980-1065, a Digambara ["sky clad," i.e., naked] monk), a Commentary on Manik Nandi's *Pareksha Mukh Sutra,* edited by Mahendra Kumar Shastri (Bombay: Nirnaya Sagar Press, 1912, 755 pp.). I am indebted to Dr. K. Sivarama of Banaras Hindu University for calling my attention to the significance of this work in the development of Bhattacharyya's thought.

60. I am indebted to Professor D. M. Datta for a summary of this untranslated work.

61. I am also indebted to Professor Datta for reading this extremely difficult work with me in a leisurely way. His own small mind, Datta remarked, nibbled a grain of truth like a squirrel nibbling a grain of corn, while Bhattacharyya's mind was like an elephant which swallows a whole jackfruit.

62. Two modes of truth in Jain logic: successive affirmation and negation distinguished from each other *(both is and is not),* simultaneous affirmation and negation rejecting an incompatible synthesis *(is indeterminate).*

63. The Jain categories part-expression *(vikaladesa)* and whole-expression *(sakaladesa).*

64. The seven truth values of Jain logic: somehow it is, is not, is indeterminate, is and is not, is and is indeterminate, is not and is indeterminate, is and is not and is indeterminate.

65. Here again, negation, rather than affirmation, is associated with existence.

66. In some respect: the category "somehow" *(syat)* of Jain logic.

67. The categories universality and particularity *(sakaladesa* and *vikaladesa)* of Jain logic.

68. *Syat,* the fundamental category of Jain logic, is not mentioned in the article and is referred to only once (I:341).

69. Translation by Kalidas Bhattacharyya.

70. *Proceedings of the First Indian Philosophical Congress, 1925* (Calcutta: Calcutta Philosophical Society, 1927), p. 133.

71. In the *Philosophical Quarterly,* edited by G. R. Malkani and published by the Indian Institute of Philosophy at Amalner, India's leading philosophical periodical from its beginning in 1925 to its cessation in 1966, which first published seven of K. C. Bhattacharyya's articles.

72. Which he also calls "reality" (not to be confused with truth).

73. Realism (that what is known need not be known) cannot be proved, but subjectivism (that what is known is constituted by the knowing) is "plainly opposed to reflective testimony" (II:131).

74. Here Bhattacharyya agrees with the classical non-dualism of Shankara.

75. The indefinite article, a concession to idiom, does not mean that the

"absolutes" are members of a class; the definite article would be more precise but might wrongly suggest one absolute with three functions.

76. Bhattacharyya also calls this (unhappily, I think) *reality* (II:142), meaning (I take it) the concrete Self not limited by its conscious contents.

77. For example: "In one direction their [the absolutes'] identity and difference are alike meaningless and in another direction their identity is intelligible though not assertable. Truth is unrelated to value, value to reality and reality to truth while value may be truth, reality value and truth reality" (II:143).

78. Based on instruction by Bhattacharyya's student Professor T. R. V. Murti, to whom I am indebted for my introduction to this doctrine. This paragraph is condensed from my "Contemporary Vedanta Philosophy," *Review of Metaphysics* 9(1955-1956):665-669.

79. These would include such pseudo-cognitive elements as forms of intuition or categories of understanding. Whatever *we impose* on the world is, strictly speaking, will, not knowledge.

80. As concrete experience not differentiated into content and consciousness, feeling may be considered psychologically as the primitive form of experience.

81. Not to be confused with concrete *experience* (feeling).

82. "The self-caused is understood in three forms—self-known, self-willed or self-felt; knowing, willing and feeling amount to self-becoming in the region of the absolute" (I:181).

83. A practical corollary is that persons desiring to reach the same goal should follow the same path.

84. "Whether a mystical identity of the absolutes can be reached in the supra-reflective consciousness does not concern us. Our problem is to show how reflection demands a specific absolute in each case" (II:128).

85. Choice among them can only be justified psychologically by individual temperament. The ways of knowing, willing, and feeling are for the intellectual, active, and artistic (*sattvika, rajasika, tamasika*) man respectively (I:173ff.). Bhattacharyya himself, his son Kalidas remarked, was "cognitive"; that was the alternative he chose, but he recognized the equal possibility of the others.

86. "There is no sense in speaking of the absolute as the unity of truth, freedom and value. It is *each* of them, these being only *spoken* separately but not *meant* either as separate or as one" (II:116).

87. The metaphysics, in turn, is determined by the philosophy of religion, and this by religion itself, according to Bhattacharyya (II:115).

88. In the order of knowing. The order of being is the reverse. "This triple absolute is apparently the prototype of the three subjective functions—knowing, willing and feeling" (II:117).

89. *Shrimant Pratapsheth Amrita Jubilee Volume* (Amalner: Indian Institute of Philosophy, 1954), vol. III, pp. 14-19.

90. A classical example of alternative absolutes is the schism in Zen Buddhism at the time of the fifth Chinese patriarch, who invited candi-

dates for the succession to submit verses. Shen-hsin wrote, "The soul is like a shining mirror; take care to keep the mirror clean"; Hui-neng retorted, "The soul is not a shining mirror; no such thing has ever been." The former presented the soul as a mirror passively reflecting, and ideally perfectly reflecting, objective Truth; the latter denied that there is any substantial soul underlying the free process of consciousness, and this became orthodox Zen. If the ideal of Truth, the mirror, was denied, it was denied not in the name of Truth but in the name of an alternative absolute.

91. Obviously meaning non-dualism; other schools of Vedanta are associated with Vaishnavism.

92. I retract my statement in "Contemporary Vedanta Philosophy" (*Review of Metaphysics* 9[1955-1956]:492) that "he has no place in his theory of knowledge for the ineffable, taking the plausible position that everything we speak is speakable." *Ineffable* properly means "speakable, but symbolically, not literally."

93. "The theory of truth . . . recognises the possibility of elaborating a primary theory of each of them" (II:117).

94. The title does not mean that the article is concerned with philosophy in general in all its three branches, although these are briefly mentioned at the end. It means that, within the context of knowing, *philosophy* is distinguished from *science*. I am indebted to Professor Rasvihary Das of the University of Calcutta for reading this article with me in 1953, as well as for first calling my attention to K. C. Bhattacharyya's philosophy.

95. London: Allen & Unwin, 1936. A second edition in 1952 added eleven younger philosophers.

96. *Absolute truth* (*Contemporary Indian Philosophy*, 2nd ed., p. 106); *the Absolute* (II:101).

97. This is the wider or symbolic use of *thought*, not synonymous with *thinking*. Only empirical facts are *literally thinkable* (II:106, 113), but the philosophical entities are objects of *thought*.

98. What is not *literally thinkable* may still be *literally spoken*, not ineffable.

99. What may be considered a long footnote to this sentence is the short article "Objective Interpretation of Percept and Image" published in the *Philosophical Quarterly* the same year. The author assumes the objective attitude to translate these subjective terms into objective terms (II:263). To *perceive* is to apprehend "a spatial object with a spatial outside," to be conscious "of a definite shape and of an outside," though the outside itself may not be definite. The object is perceived as *existent* when it defines its outside. This occurs when the object appears, as a scar on a man's face when he approaches—the object emerging in time but existing in space—or disappears, as a flame going out—the field emerging in time but the object existing in space. To have an incipient *image* is to know an object as persistent but not as existent (II:266). To have an

image proper is to know an object as persistent and not existent (II:267). Existence and persistence are the objective interpretations of percept and image respectively.

100. Philosophy, consequently, is neither a speculative world-view or synthesis of sciences nor a critical examination of the structure of science (II:109).

101. Or, at any rate, the non-ego, if the word *object* is taken to involve reference to subject (I:151).

102. Or, as he would put it, their indeterminate togetherness.

103. Cf.: "It is not objective being but objective negation or freedom that is eternally willed" (II:295).

104. Of the four principal Hindu philosophies, the metaphysically oriented Vedanta, scientifically oriented Sankhya, psychologically oriented Yoga, and logically oriented Nyaya, Bhattacharyya wrote studies on all except the last. This is perhaps to be regretted, as Nyaya, already exquisitely subtle in its classical form would seem an especially fertile field for his peculiar talents.

105. He "has almost at every cardinal point turned Sankhya into a living and original thought," says Kalidas Bhattacharyya (*Memorial Volume*, p. 230).

106. *Free being* and *active quiescence* are paradoxical combinations of contradictory terms.

107. That is, Freedom, related to willing as Truth to knowing.

108. Abstention from vice, practice of virtue, body control, breath control, introversion, concentration, meditation, *samadhi*.

109. We know that God must exist but not that he does exist (I:320).

110. Not to be confused with intuition. God is "a postulate of the contemplative attitude and not the content of knowledge."

111. It may presuppose a moral and religious discipline, and religious activity may be an alternative procedure, coordinate with Yoga procedure, either leading to *samadhi* (I:305).

112. The Four Noble Truths of Buddhism. If I interpret this difficult paragraph correctly, it would seem, though the author does not say so, that Buddhism and Yoga propose alternative forms of absolute Freedom.

113. For *the child* read *of distinction* (I:350, 5th line from bottom).

114. Compare P. J. Chaudhury, *Studies in Aesthetics* (Calcutta: Rabindra Bharati, 1964), p. 23: "Indian aestheticians do not consider beauty as an objective reality so much. They deal with the perception of the beautiful which is an enjoyed characteristic like taste or flavour (*rasa*) rather than a substantive entity."

115. *Studies in Kant* were published the following year.

116. Analogous distinctions between Truth as reflection of outer reality or assertion of inner reality and Freedom as detachment or creation might generate a system of six alternative forms of the Absolute, three objective and three subjective.

117. For Kalidas Bhattacharyya's recollection of these conversations

five years after his father's death see my article "Contemporary Vedanta Philosophy" (*Review of Metaphysics* 9[1955-1956]:494-496).

118. Calcutta: Das Gupta, 1953, 366 pp. The logic of alternation is applied to various problems of psychology, logic, metaphysics, aesthetics, ethics, and politics in an earlier book *Object Content and Relation* (Calcutta: Das Gupta, n.d., 160 pp.) and several articles in *Calcutta Review, Entretiens, K. C. Bhattacharyya Memorial Volume, Our Heritage, Philosophical Quarterly, Philosophy East and West, Proceedings of the Indian Philosophical Congress, The Mother,* and *Visvabharati Quarterly.* Analysis of these works is beyond the scope of the present article.

119. *Object Content and Relation,* p. 141.

120. In a conversation held on March 26, 1961.

121. "There are then three alternative ideals of life—duty, right and love," says Kalidas Bhattacharyya, "Alternative Forms of Politics," *Calcutta Review,* 3rd series: 86(1943):37.

122. H. R. Isaacs, quoted in *A.A.U.P. Bulletin* 52(1966):52.

Place of the
Indefinite in Logic

Place of the
Indefinite in Logic

1. The purpose of this paper is to examine what modifications of logical doctrine would be necessitated by the admission of the indefinite in logic, side by side with definite position and definite negation. In logic which ordinarily deals with the definite content of thought only, the indefinite is considered in at least three ways. It may be regarded explicitly as extralogical, as only something subjective or psychological which it is the purpose of the science to outgrow or supersede. Sometimes it is treated as provisionally definite; both the uncertain and certain relation of the knowing faculty to the object is taken to yield definite forms of positive logic, the indefinite in fact being admitted as only an epistemological element of the definite content of logic.[1] In dialectic, it is taken as definite function of truth itself, as the *function* of negation which is neither a mere epistemological element nor a static truth by itself but still a constructive factor of definite truth only. Our inquiry is whether and how logic should find place for the absolute indefinite as distinct from the indefinite that is only constitutive of the definite and our prima facie justification for the inquiry is that there is such a thing as a metaphysic of absolute doubt—at least a philosophy of the irrational—and that logic as the prolegomena to all science and

metaphysics should not commit itself to the particular metaphysical faith in the finality of a definite system of truth. The indefinite has found in fact a place in metaphysics in many forms. To mention only a few at random, there is the "negative" matter of Plato, the māyā of the Vedāntists, and the śūnyam or 'void' of the Buddhists. There is the notion of objective chance in Aristotle and of the inexplicable change of direction of the atoms of Lucretius. There is the conception of the indeterminate will, specially in the extreme form of unmotived or irrational activity, as presented by a Duns Scotus, a Schopenhauer, or a Bergson, and there is finally the Unknowable whether of Kant or of Spencer. These notions are at present homeless in logic; there is no category to express them and disputes arise in connection with them in metaphysic which properly should have arisen in logic itself.

2. It is necessary to begin by clearly defining the scope of logic as conceived here. Whatever may have been the origin of the science, in its present state it can hardly be treated except mainly as a positive science distinct alike from psychology and the objective sciences and concerned with the most abstract principles, not only of all science, but of all philosophy. It deals with the object or content of all knowledge claimed as such and in this sense is an objective science, though the object here means all thinkables, subjective, objective, and absolute. It considers only the form of the object, not the matter and so its primary problem should be whether there is any form which is not matter, which is not determinate, which is undeniably presupposed in all determinate concrete thought, accepted or disputed, which in fact—paradoxical as it may sound—is not affected even by the uncertainty of this problem. It is not the primary purpose of logic to develop this form, if it can be discovered, into the ground-principles or categories of the several concrete departments of thought. That would be committing oneself to a particular system of metaphysic; and logic, as prior to all metaphysic, can only indicate these by way of bringing out all that it does not deal with. For purposes of logic, in other words, it should be assumed that all intuitions that are claimed as such and all sciences and philosophies *may* be true; it must be universal in the sense not only of presenting the form common to all that is claimed as knowledge but also as presenting the form of all doubt and dispute.

3. This view of logic is forced upon us by the circumstance that it has to take account not only of the positive sciences but also of metaphysics. Metaphysics in reopening the fundamental questions assumed to be settled in the sciences presents many alternative solutions of which it is not for logic to accept or reject any on the ground of common sense, for the whole purpose of the science is to replace the rough-and-ready rule of the thumb. A similar problem gave rise to epistemology as a prolegomena to all branches of knowledge claimed as such but there is this difference from logic as we conceive it here that it itself represents a body of knowledge that is determinate or uncriticized, resting as it does either on the authority of introspection or on that of traditional logic for the solution of the critical problem without a prior criticism of these authorities themselves. This prior criticism, if undertaken, would yield us logic proper, with its absolutely abstract or fundamental character. If epistemology has not been able so far to maintain its role of a prolegomena and has come to be a mere chapter in some metaphysical system, dialectical or other, it is because it has not stripped itself, to start with, of all determinate presuppositions, because in fact it has not been fundamental enough. That the transcendental logic of Kant, for example, led to the positive dialectic logic of Hegel only shows that the antithesis between the transcendental and positive is not absolute in the sphere of the determinate. In both, the abstractions with which logic is taken to be conversant are taken to be constructive functions: they are viewed as at once analytic and synthetic. In Kant, the analytic moment indeed remains transcendental in view of a consciousness of a limit to reason, of an indefinite thing-in-itself; but this consciousness of the indefinite is not taken seriously to affect the epistemology itself. The definite unity of the self and its synthetic specification into a definite system of categories are obviously suggested by the presuppositions of a particular system of metaphysic, namely, the developmental, and the indefinite itself is taken to be *real* without criticism. Logic in our present conception, however, in endeavoring to supply the abstract form of epistemological knowledge itself would stand on a height of abstraction where the distinction of the transcendental positive is obliterated. The synthetic developmental principle has no necessary place in it any more than the principle of determinate identity, for it has no right to build on

a determinate metaphysical presupposition: the principle of logic should be absolutely abstract.

4. Can we have such a science at all? If we demand a criticism of epistemology, should we not demand a criticism of the criticism and so on ad infinitum? Epistemology starts with a principle that it believes to be self-evident or necessary. If, however, a real doubt is cast on the principle, if the basis of intuition or axiom in general is challenged as it has been challenged, logic as such has no right to enter into the dispute and to take sides; and so on in criticizing epistemology, it cannot stand on any so-called necessary or self-evident principle. To start with a determinate contingent principle would be equally absurd and so it can only stand on an indeterminate principle which can indifferently be called necessary or contingent. This principle can be no other than the bare dualism of the definite and indefinite, in which neither has even the specific implication of reality or unreality. A further criticism of this dualism is unintelligible, for the negation of the principle is nothing other than the principle itself.

5. To explicate this principle. The most abstract and comprehensive dualism that can be conceived is that between the definite and the indefinite. It is possible to show in the case of any other dualism that can be proposed that there is a *third* something beyond it. Even in the case of being and non-being, one can cite an indefinite that is neither, call it the unknowable or freedom or whatever else. It is not necessary to present the dualism of definite and indefinite in the form of a judgment as a law of thought, for the law-form is only a form among forms: the judgment is not the necessary logical unit in such logic as is conceived here. But if a law-form is demanded for this principle—the word "principle" is sufficiently general in philosophical usage, it may be presented in the paradoxical form—the indefinite is not and is indefinite at once. It is similar to the dialectical principle of the identity of being and not-being but there is the difference that in the latter, more stress is laid in the last resort on the identity than on the difference between the opposed terms: the synthesis of position and negation is uncritically taken to be only positive, and the final synthesis, namely, the absolute, is taken as a positive system of truth. In the principle we have presented, equal stress is laid on the identity and difference of the opposed terms; what it amounts to is that the line between the definite and the indefinite is itself

indefinite and that the minimum of difference from the indefinite that constitutes the abstract definite is a vanishing quantity.

6. The difference from the dialectical principle can be stated in another way. The ground principle of logic has been formulated in at least three ways—in the form of system or reason, in the form of relation or judgment, and in the form of an irrelative term, intuition or experience. The identity of being and non-being points to the conception of system as the ruling conception of dialectic. In conceptualist or intuitionist logic, the fundamental principle is best conceived as a relation between positive terms, that is, as an ordinary judgment like "this being is not another being." In empirical logic, an experience is the test of its own truth and so the basal principle may be formulated as "this determinate being *Mill* or this determinate becoming *Bain* which is not non-being." In the principle proposed for the logic of the indefinite, no preference is implied for any of these three forms. It is best put as a mere dualism or opposition, definite *and* indefinite, the "and" expressing apparently the very form of illogicality or the despair of knowledge. It really however expresses the inadequacy of the three forms aforesaid. As against the form of reason, the dialectical principle, it indicates an alternative—unreason—beyond reason: position and negation are not necessarily the moments of the positive absolute. As against the form of judgment, the conceptualist principle as we may call it, it suggests that beyond determinate affirmation and negation, there is the indeterminate (though it may be practically useful) form of doubt or ignorance. As against the form of the irrelative determinate term—we call it the experimental principle provisionally—it points out that the positive object of experience is always a determination carved out of the indeterminate. It suggests, in fact, that the indefinite has to be recognized as standing outside the term, the judgment, and the inference, that one should go beyond ordinary logic which simply turns its back on the outlying indefinite and looks to the definite as the sole content of thought.

7. Such recognition of the indefinite implies not only an extension of logical doctrine: it involves also a material modification of the logic of the definite. With regard to the term, for example, the determinate object of experience, our principle shows that the boundaries that demarcate it from the surrounding indefinite are

themselves indefinite or indefinable, that the particularity of "this determinate" is something unique which can neither be taken as a separate definite category nor as a necessary determination of the universal and accordingly the "this" may be indifferently taken as either being (Mill) or as transition (Bain).[2] With regard to the judgment-form, it is pointed out that definite relation, affirmative and negative, is itself indefinite, that if relation is given fact, the "givenness" is an indeterminate which can be regarded either as an abrupt positive or as a negation of the indefinite and that the negation of the indefinite is indifferently affirmative or negative, that is, the distinction between affirmative and negative is indefinable or in other words, contradiction is just as conceivable as otherwise.[3] With regard to the form of reasoning, our principle would indicate that system or necessary relation is as much a given fact as a negation of negation and that this negation of negation may be taken as equivalent to position or negation indifferently.[4]

8. With the Hegelians then, we admit the identity of being and non-being or necessity but hold that this necessity is itself a contingent fact. So the contradiction between being and non-being is to us as much an object of thought as their non-contradiction; a contradictory judgment is neither inadmissible nor is merely a moment in the necessity of dialectical identity. So, too, the determinate *this* has not simply being and negation in its constitution but also the indefinite or the Unknowable.

9. The indeterminate being or non-being with which Hegel starts is not the same as our indefinite. In the term, "this determinate," "this" is something unique to which neither the terms, "being" or non-being can be applied, though "thisness" or determinate being may be taken as an identity of being and non-being. As constitutive of "thisness" then, the indeterminate being or non-being of Hegel is still definite in our sense: "this" as transcending "thisness" is unanalyzable, indefinable, or indefinite. "This determinate" may thus be analyzed into the three principles—the indefinite, being, and non-being. In reference to the criticism of the Hegelian position that logic should start with determinate being rather than with pure being, we hold that the indefinite, being, and non-being can all be taken as the starting point indifferently, these being all implied in "this determinate."

10. With reference to the judgment, our contention is that it is

equally true to say that the terms are or are not constituted by their relation, that in it a given matter of fact, a "this" which is neither definite being nor definite non-being is determined into a relation of terms, that the relation is at once identity and difference in reference to this indefinite, and that apart from this indefinite, it is just as true to say that there is as that there is not necessary mutual implication between identity and difference, that the affirmative relation is and that it is not prior to the negative.[5] As to reasoning, the necessity implied in the "therefore" is taken by Hegel as the self-creating dialectic of truth itself, as the position created by the negation of negation. In empirical logic, it is taken to be the position contingently reached through other positions, as a particular reached through particulars; and in conceptualist logic, it is the mere explication of a position by negation, as a rendering of a universal premise analytically definite by an individualizing minor premise. We, however, hold that the new something reached in the conclusion is really a definition of the indefinite matter to which reasoning has reference and that the necessity is but a contingent fact in this reference.

11. Hegelian Logic does not admit the indefinite but holds instead that dialectic necessity is creative. Its strength lies however only in *seeing* that a real category of given experience *was* necessary, not really in yielding any new category or creating it. Hence where it has sought to create, critics have only seen a dismal failure or found that it was a sort of prophesying after the event. This inability to create is, in fact, the implicit admission of the indefinite. What the critics do not bring out however is that this retrospective prophecy, this *seeing* that a stage which has emerged *was* necessary is a true seeing: they have yet to explain why the dialectic exposition which is not at least explicitly analytic *fits* the category deduced, how an apparent continuity between an old and a new category is at all established by the mere process of negation of negation. It is a form of the old question how what is anticipated by inference comes to be verified by experience and to call it a mere accident or to understand a preestablished harmony is simply to give up the problem of explanation.

12. At the same time it is true that such anticipations of inference are not sometimes verified, that only probable truths are

reached actually by inference and hence the justification for taking the inferential form as only an ideal and for distinguishing it from the material process of inference itself. This amounts on the one hand to the admission of the analytic necessity within this ideal form as itself *given* and as *somehow* applicable to the indefinite matter of experience and on the other to the view that the synthetic material process is a definite necessity inexplicably emerging out of the indefinite. In conceptualist logic, the definite analytic necessity within the syllogism is understood as the given or intuited ideal and error or uncertainty is taken as only the accident of application. In empirical logic where the ideal is nothing and the material process is all, it only amounts to saying that *somehow* as a matter of fact we pass from particulars to other particulars which are sometimes verified.

13. As against conceptualist logic, Kant holds that the forms of positive logic are not merely given but are synthetic apriori necessities at bottom, that their applicability to experience is not accidental but necessary, that however although matter in general is necessarily demanded by form, *what* specifically the matter will be is unknowable. The Kantian view thus brings out the latent implication of the indefinite in the intuited character and applicability of the forms admitted in conceptualist logic. As against empirical logic, Spencer points out that unless logic is to lapse into psychology, the ideal form has to be taken as necessarily presupposed in the material process, that inference is inference only as implying the consciousness of justification or necessary ground, that this necessary ground or axiom is not only the consolidation of contingent experiences but has the implication of the inconceivability of the opposite and that experience taken as the *given* definite in empirical logic is really the indefinite breaking forth into the relation of difference.

14. Both Kant and Spencer thus bring out the transcendent character of the indefinite but both uncritically take this indefinite to be the unknowable *reality*. Against this however we hold that the indefinite may as well be called the unknowable negation, that in fact it is a third category side by side with position and negation, that it is as much immanent in the definite as transcendent, and that therefore it is not simply the transcendental implicate of definite logic but the content of positive logic itself.

15. Our logic thus finds categories for widely different

metaphysical notions of reality, for the notion of the knowable world as unreal in the last resort as well as for the notion of it as a real evolute in all different senses in which it has been taken. Logic as here conceived renders intelligible the denial of the unique positive reality of the given, not only in the sense in which Hegel understands it who admits the reality and takes it to be constructed by negation, but also in the absolute sense. The assertion of the ultimate falsity of the world—falsity not only to absolute intuition but to logical thought itself—is thus conceivable. In positive logic itself, not only is position to be conceived as negation of negation as it is conceived in dialectic: it is to be admitted also that negation of negation may be indefinite negation. At the same time we recognize that the indefinite may be regarded as real and as embodied in the definite axioms and experiences that we start with as positively *given*. We admit the truth both of conceptualist and empirical logic or—what is the same thing—we can conceive the metaphysical view that determinate noumena or phenomena or both side by side constitute the knowable world. There is nothing finally to prevent us from conceiving that this immanent being is to the transcendent real indefinite a real mode, effect, or objectification, that the definite is a real specification of the indefinite. We thus frankly make a positive use, logical and metaphysical, of the indefinite, unlike Kant and Spencer who while deprecating such positive use of the indefinite view it implicitly as the *real*. Conflicting epistemological notions are also thus logically conceivable: both necessity and fact can be understood alike as an emanation and evolute of the indefinite, and each may be regarded as the other—that is, necessity may be taken as an inexplicable fact, as the positive stress of the indefinite real and given fact may be viewed as implying negation of an indefinite negation.

16. The general implications of our principle—the indefinite and definite are and are not one—have been brought out as demarcating the logic of the indefinite from other types of logic. The bearing of it on some details taken at random may be discussed by way of further elucidation.

17. *Conception of "all" and "some."* Logic as dealing with the most abstract content of thought, definite and indefinite, has no direct interest in developing the determinate categories of the several departments of knowledge. If it refers to quantity then, even in the vague form of "all" and "some," it is only by way of

bringing out what it does not deal with. The primary question is whether it starts with the determinate or the indeterminate and our answer is that the starting point is "this determinate," where "this" is the unique indefinite. The difference of the definite and indefinite being itself indefinable, the difference of the determinates from one another is also indeterminate in the last resort. From the side of the definite as fixed by language, we deny this indeterminate difference which we are conscious of, by using the word "all": the connotation is primarily meant as definite, in view however of the indeterminate differences of the particulars constituting the denotation. The word "some" on the contrary primarily means this indeterminate difference in view of the definite connotation. The secondary accompaniment in each case is affected by the primary intention. We have said that the definite and the indefinite are not only different but identical and so the indefinite denotation of "all A"—indefinite as fixed by connotation and not by enumeration—is itself a definite function or form in logic: and the definite connotation of "some A"—namely, the connotation of A—is itself rendered indefinite, "some A" being equivalent to "all A x" where x is an indefinite determination of A. Insofar then as we say that the definite is *not* the indefinite, subalternation may be regarded as an opposition and not so insofar as we admit their identity: the truth of "all" both denies and admits the truth of "some."[6] This only means that quantity-difference which is the object or content of thought and not merely psychological is itself indefinite and that these contradictory views about "all" and "some" may be both true. Logic should consider this fact of alternation only: it should not be its business to develop the quantitative doctrine itself into some sort of logical algebra or geometry. Nor is it its business to settle the psychological or metaphysical question of the concept, although in thus defining its own business, it would indirectly indicate the germs of the concrete solutions of the question that have been presented.

18. *Negative conditional propositions.* Can conditional propositions be negative? (1) There are the opposite views about the hypothetical proposition—(a) As distinct from the categorical, its sole function is to express the logical or objective dependence of one relation on another. Non-dependence is no objective relation at all and requires no logical form to express it. The consciousness of it is purely privative: that I cannot connect a consequent with

an antecedent is a mere subjective incapacity. There is therefore no negative hypothetical. (b) It may be contended however that in any case the negative categorical is allowed in this view (we need not discuss the extreme view according to which no negative relation is admitted in logic), that is, the negative relation is admitted as objective, though with the implied assumption that it is equivalent to a definite affirmative which may not be known yet. As a logical form then, the negative categorical is admissible where subjectively there is the ignorance of its affirmative equivalent. Now there should be a difference between the dependence of an affirmative consequent and that of a negative consequent on a given antecedent. The quality of the dependence itself varies with the quality of the consequent and hence a negative hypothetical should be admitted if a negative categorical is admitted. To be negative the hypothetical need not express nondependence but only dependence of a negation.

19. The dispute here really turns on whether the quality of the dependence is affected by the quality of the consequent. Where we do not know yet what affirmation is equivalent to the negative consequent, should we say that the hypothetical proposition itself is negative? Should we express the state of knowledge there by a hypothetical form at all? We take the example—"if the keys cannot be found in this room after so much search, they are not here." I do not know *where* the keys are then and still it may be useful to express the circumstance in the negative hypothetical form: I need not waste time searching for it in this room for the reason stated. But it is urged in the first view that what is expressed in this proposition is only something subjective: there is no objective connection between the antecedent and the consequent, the absence of the keys here being not conditioned by the fruitless search. But this only means that the keys have not been removed from the room in consequence of the fruitless search. The absence of the keys need not however mean this positive removal and may yet be a useful truth that is inferred from, that is, is conditioned by the fruitless search as its reason or ground. It is not the content of mere ignorance. Mere ignorance, it may be said, need not be expressed in logic: what is called the privative judgment in logic is *useless*. The proposition about the keys is useful and yet is not the expression of an objective dependence of a positive fact. Should this intermediate state of consciousness between mere ignorance and positive objective knowledge be

expressed in logic? Venn has pointed out the fallacy of over-objectification in logic: to him, logic deals with the *passage* from the subjective to the objective. We hold that logic as dealing with object in the abstract sense of content of thought can never *over*-objectify and that the real truth of Venn's view is that logic deals with the passage from the indefinite to the definite in the object. The useful knowledge about the keys which is not yet positive objective knowledge has a content or object distinct alike from the absolutely indefinite and useless content of ignorance and from the definite object of the positive knowledge of the whereabouts of the keys: it is at once indefinite and definite and as such should have a logical expression. The logic of the indefinite would therefore admit the negative hypothetical and point out that its logical status is indefinite—somewhere intermediate between the forms of positive knowledge and absolute ignorance, and a stage removed in point of definiteness from the negative categorical judgment. The negative categorical is already the explicit objective embodiment of partial ignorance: it assigns a provisional being to negation in relation to a position. In an affirmative hypothetical also, the *contingent* being of the relation in the consequent is such an explicit objective embodiment of partial ignorance: the assertory being of the categorical relation is modified by a negation into a possibility. The negative hypothetical then is an objective embodiment of a double ignorance or negation but is still in view of a position and therefore useful.

20. It may be noted in passing that the issues here are similar to those which arise in the Vedāntic discussion of the illusion of illusion.[7] An illusion being positively *given* has an "indescribable being" according to Vedānta, even when it is corrected. Has the illusion of illusion such a being also? A compromise between plain yes and no is given by some Vedāntists, namely, that the illusion of illusion is *given* in a way different from, that is, more indefinitely than illusion itself. A similar difficulty may be pressed against Bradley's view of the negative judgment. It presupposes, he says, not a full-formed affirmative judgment but only a question. What is the nature of the question? He himself takes it to be *only psychological,* an ideal suggestion, a floating idea. Bosanquet however would take it as a logical content, a rudimentary disjunction. Sigwart would call it a rudimentary positive judgment—that is, a merely *given* relation. They all admit that a

full affirmative judgment need not be presupposed by the negative and yet *what* precisely do they contend about? It is really somewhere intermediate between the *content* of thought and the mere psychological *fact* of thought. This transitional something between the definitely psychological and the definitely logical can only be taken cognizance of in such logic as has been conceived in this paper.

21. (2) As to the disjunctive proposition, the ordinary view is that it cannot be negative in the disjunctive form. The definite element in "A is either B or C" is that A is in B and C taken together and sometimes the definite side is pushed further to imply the mutual exclusion of B and C. There is indefiniteness then at least as to *which* of the two, B and C, is predicated of A: the disjunctive is so far an explicit embodiment of partial ignorance. It would be held then that "A is either not B or not C" is not the logical denial of "A is either B or C," for if the ignorance-element in both is considered, there is no denial, an indefinite being only *indefinitely* related to an indefinite, and if the knowledge-element in both is considered, B plus C is either the same as or a part of not-B plus not-C. In reference to the knowledge-element however, we intend to point out as in the case of subalternation that if the connotative side as distinct from the denotative side of B and C is considered, there is an intelligible sense in which B plus C may be taken as the negative of not-B plus not-C.

22. Those who hold that "A is either B or C" do not deny that A may be both really point to this connotative side: the precise relation between the denotations of B and C may remain indefinite according to them when the disjunctive is asserted. From this standpoint then "either not B or not C" would be doubly indeterminate. In "A is either B or C," it is only affirmed that the connotations of B and C are compatible with that of A. This compatibility is a definite logical content but the mutual relation of B and C understood connotatively is indefinite; the mutual relation of not-B and not-C then would be doubly indefinite. The problem is to find out the value of this double indefiniteness.

23. We may distinguish our position here from at least four positions that may be conceivably advanced. (1) It may be held that the negation of the indefinite "either B or C" in the form "either not-B or not-C" has nothing definite in it and is absolutely useless. (2) There is just the opposite view that "either not-B or not-C" is the same as "either B or C," B and C being already

exclusive. (3) Or it may be held that the mutual exclusion of B and C is indefinite in "either B or C," and that "either not-B or not-C" makes this definite, that it amounts to a more definite affirmation and is therefore no *negation* at all; it is *extra* affirmation, an *added* truth *side by side* with the definite truth of "either B or C." Or (4) it may be urged that this extra affirmation is a *development* of "either B or C" rather than an accretion, that it is undoubtedly a negation but amounting to an affirmation. "Either not-B or not-C" is taken as (1) no logical form at all or (2) as identical with "either B or C" or (3) as different from it but not a denial of it or (4) as a denial of it that amounts to a definite affirmation which is at once same and different. Our position however is that "either not-B or not-C" is the form of the *indefinite denial* of "either B or C." It is denial of the definite element in it—namely, the compatibility of B and of C with A: that the compatibility itself is partial or indefinite, is *not* definite, is pointed out by "A is either not B or not C." As the denial of what is believed to be a definite element in "A is either B or C," it is itself *believed* in and is not dumb ignorance: it has a useful content which yet is not positive, not the same as the given affirmative nor something coordinate with it, nor a negation amounting to a definite positive.

24. That "A is either not B or not C" is the negation of "A is either B or C" may be shown in another way. The ordinary form given of its negation is "A is neither B nor C." This however states more than the mere negation which should be simply "A *may* be neither." If not-B and not-C are understood as the negation of the connotative side of B and C, "A is either not-B or not-C" is equivalent to "A is either B or C or neither," which means precisely that A may be neither.

25. In speaking of a logical form being useful, we have assumed only for the sake of the argument that the merely privative judgment, the expression of mere ignorance, is useless. It is necessary now to point out that the word "useful" is itself a question-begging term: it dogmatically assumes that the knowing self ought to move toward more and more determinate truth. This assumption itself may be questioned and the logical impulse may be taken to be satisfied in the correction of the given error of determinateness, not in the attainment of new determinations, in getting rid of the limitation of the definite and not in securing increase of definiteness, in the direction of the indefinite and not

in that of the definite—freedom or the absolute state being reached either way. In this "undefining" process, as we may call it, it is not even necessary that empirical truth should be held fast provisionally. All doubt, including what is taken to be the most irresponsible form of it—namely, absolute skepticism, would be *useful* in this connection, though there might be grades of usefulness here also. Logic, conceived to deal with the bare dualism of the definite and indefinite, can make room for either kind of usefulness or truth.

26. This may be presented in terms of the disjunctive proposition. The proposition "A is either B or C or neither" may be taken as equivalent to "A is either B or not-B," the bare form of the Excluded Middle. Now this form may be taken (1) as absolutely useless, a joke, the mere form of ignorance; (2) as the limiting form of disjunction, and therefore a particular case of disjunction, giving us the form of truth, that is, of the universe as constructed by thought out of the unique given; (3) as the form of the determinate—determinate position and negation as coordinate—present in all particular disjunctions; or (4) as the abstract form of truth *developed* in all concrete disjunctions, in all grades of determinate knowledge. Not-B in these views is (1) nothing logical at all, (2) logical only in relation to the unique but definite "givenness" of B, (3) a positive logical content side by side with B, and (4) the logical implication of B, as B is of not-B. In conformity to what we have said above, we hold that not-B is something logical, though not definite: it is the logical useful indefinite. "A is either B or not-B" is a logical negative of "A is either B or C"; utterly indeterminate in contrast with it but determinate as expressing the fundamental logical principle of the disjunction of the definite and indefinite, the form of the knowable-unknowable, the form of mystery rather than of absolute truth, the limiting mystery of all philosophy.

NOTES

1. See ref. to Venn, *Symbolic Logic*, 1881, 19.
2. Within empiricism in fact is reproduced the opposition between the conceptualistic and dialectic views of the *principium individuationis*. To conceptualist logic, individuality as such is properly a unique category of thought, a simple ultimate thought, and there is sometimes a tendency

to abolish it altogether. To dialectic, it is a construction through thought as a function. (i) In the empiricism of Mill, corresponding to the simple *thought* of "this," appears "this" individual experience, this given simple being. (ii) In Bain however, experience is taken to be a transition; properly no term is given but only a passage, a differentiation between terms. Individuality is only an arbitrary point in this transitional process; it is a conflux of relations or generalities. Existence is admitted as a separate category, distinct from coexistence, sequence, and resemblance by Mill but not by Bain. These conflicting views only show that the unit-term or the individual is at once definite and indefinite, the latter aspect being systematically ignored in ordinary logic.

3. Here within conceptualism is reproduced the opposition between empirical and dialectical views of *relation*. To empiricism, relation is a given experience; the elementary relations of likeness and difference are taken as ultimate feelings. To dialectic, it is the *function* of negation, the negation of immediacy, the self-distinction of the given. The conceptualist view splits up into at least two types: (i) relation is an ultimate given thought and here the ultimate difference between empiricism and intuitionism is a vanishing one. All relation in fact is positive; negation itself is but positive difference. (ii) Positive relation and negative relation are coordinate: absence or void is a category side by side with existence. The given positive stands over against its definite negation: the primary difference is not difference between two positives but between position and negation, this negation being thus a sort of being or position. Thus the distinction between affirmation and negation becomes indefinable. Negation is not being and yet a sort of being. These conflicting views show again that what is taken to be definite relation in ordinary logic is really indefinite.

4. The opposition between empiricism and conceptualism has to be traced as affecting the integrity of the dialectic view of *system* or necessary relation. To empiricism, system is no given being: the past does not *exist* in the present and yet the present is what it is *because* of the past. The ground of present knowledge is always non-existent. To conceptualism, the relation of ground and consequent is an eternally existent thought. The dialectic movement presents both these tendencies without reconciling them. As the ground of itself (natura naturans), it is a transition, negation of negation, freedom—no existent being. As the consequence of itself (natura naturata), it is the *existent* absolute, the *truth* that is thought through and through. This alternation of the dynamic and static aspects in dialectic points to the fact that system or reason is indefinite in its very constitution.

5. The judgment "A is B" has been understood in at least three ways: (i) A does not exist when A B exists. (ii) A exists when A B exists. (iii) A exists *because* A B does not exist but is a function—the empirical, conceptualist, and dialectic views respectively in typical form. Taking (ii), A is in the limit the unique "this," transcending the determination A B. As

indeterminate, it is as much definite being as negation and thus (i) is justified along with (ii). So in (iii), A B, the function or negation, *is*, i.e., constitutes A, the existent. Thus A or "this" is negation, being, and their identity in (i), (ii), (iii) respectively: it is in (i) the not-given (not-now-given), in (ii) the given, and in (iii) the existent through not being given. A B then is (i) not A, (ii) is not A and yet is A, and (iii) is A by being not A; in other words, the negative relation is *after* the affirmative, *coordinate with* the affirmative and *before* the affirmative in the three views.—All these variations of view point to the circumstance that relation is at once definite and indefinite: the admission of the indefinite justifies and falsifies all these views.

6. There are the two ordinary views: (i) "some" means *not* "all"; (ii) some does not deny "all"—i.e., (i) some is a definite negation of "all," (ii) "some" is indefinite. In both views, "some" is taken as both definite and indefinite in a sense, e.g., in (i) though it means "not all," it is indefinite which individuals and how many are meant.—Still it is held that this indefiniteness is only subjective: to logic, it means the definite "not all," definite because "not all A" means "all Ax"—i.e., the connotation of A as qualified by an unknown but real adjective x. In (ii), though "some" is indefinite as not denying "all," it means definitely at least one individual having the connotation of the class: the indefinite is thus provisionally treated as definite in logic. The second view does not assume what the first does that "some A" is necessarily equivalent to *another* universal, viz., Ax; and the first does not assume what the second does that any individual A is definitely known to have the predicate B in the judgment "some A is B." The first would assert "some A is B" on the two definite grounds (1) that at least one individual A has been found to be *not* B and (2) that therefore the real connection of B is not with A but with Ax. The second would assert it on the ground (1) that at least one A *is* B and (2) that other A's are either B or not B. The first emphasizes the defect of connotation (A should be determined into Ax), i.e., the indefiniteness of the connotation which is taken to be definite in "all A" and the second emphasizes the indefiniteness of the denotation in "some A" which is already indefinite in "all A," though the point is provisionally ignored there. "All A" in fact is both definite and indefinite, definite in connotation and indefinite in denotation. "Some A," as *indefinite in connotation* (A—Ax) is a negation of "all A"; but "some A," as indefinite in denotation, is no negation of "all A," the indefinite being indefinitely related to the indefinite.—The recognition of the indefinite as a logical, and not merely a subjective, element brings out the truth of both the views of "some" and "all." The logic of the indefinite thus not only makes conflicting logical doctrines intelligible: it points out the essential indeterminateness of the concept, and the really extralogical character of quantity—showing that logic is here uselessly racked with disputes about what as outside its scope must be disputed and indicating that the doctrine of quantity is capable of being developed, not only from the side

of the determinate but also from that of the indeterminate.

7. Something is believed to be real it is next taken to be illusory, and then again on closer observation it may be pronounced *not* illusory. What does "not illusory" mean?

The Subject as Freedom

Chapter 1
The Notion of Subjectivity

1. Object is what is meant, including the object of sense-perception and all contents that have necessary reference to it. Object as the meant is distinguished from the subject or the subjective of which there is some awareness other than the meaning-awareness. The subjective cannot be a *meaningless* word: to be distinguished from, it must be a significant speakable and yet if it be a meant content, it would be but object. It can thus neither be asserted nor denied to be a meant content and what cannot be denied need not be assertable. Apparently, the significant speakable is wider than the meanable: a content to be communicated and understood need not be meant.

2. A meaning that is conveyed by a word must be intelligible to the hearer as what he would himself convey by the word. What the speaker means by a word must be capable of being meant by the hearer if he were to use it. The word *this* as used by a speaker means primarily what he perceives; and although the hearer may use it of some other object, he can use it of the same object. A general term is always understood by the speaker and the hearer to mean the same thing but such identity of the general meaning is possible only because it applies to the same individual thing, the same perceived *this* to both. The word *this* may accordingly be taken as the symbol of the object or what is meant.

3. The word *I* as used by a speaker is not understood by the hearer to convey what he would himself convey by the use of it. If he used the word, he would intend himself and not the speaker. Actually, however, when he understands the word *I* as used by the speaker, he understands it to stand for the speaker. He may accordingly be said to understand the thing intended by the speaker through the word but not through the *meaning* of the word. The thing is not meant by the word for the further reason that the communicating act of the speaker which is never a part of the meaning of a word is itself conveyed by the word *I*. When the object-consciousness of the speaker is communicated, the object and not the speaking of the object is what is understood to be meant. But when his self-consciousness is communicated, it is not his self only but the self as speaking, communicating, or expressing itself that is understood. His self-consciousness may in this sense be said to be not merely expressed but *incarnated* in the word *I*. What is here intended by the speaker is not only what the hearer can never intend by the word if he were to use it: it is also the thing-subject—*as expressing itself* and not as merely expressed. What then is meant and is expressible as *this* is not what is conveyed by the word *I*.

4. Object as symbolized by the word *this* may be an individual object or a generality. The word *I* as intending the subject is not definitely either singular or general. It is indeed *used* to indicate not only one thing at a time but a thing which cannot be indicated by more than one speaker; but then different speakers can be *understood* to use it—each of a distinct thing, namely, himself—by the same hearer and understood to use as he would use it. As used, the term has a uniquely singular reference; but as understood, it is general in the sense the term *unique* is general. It is thus unlike a term meaning an objective content, which has the same reference—singular or general—to the speaker as to the hearer. What is meant by *this* is distinct from what is intended by *I*, though the latter may be intended or indicated by *this*. The object is not the subject but the subject may be spoken of though not meant as object. The subject may be incarnated in the spoken word *I* which is objective. As incarnated in the object, the subject is the object which yet is distinct from it. In terms of *I* and *this*, we may say that the statement "this is I" is false while the statement "I am this" cannot be denied.

5. If *this* stands for a perceivable object including my body, there is no occasion to make the statement "this is I" or "I am this." But *this* may stand for myself who *spoke* the word *I*; and in answer to the conceivable question "who is this speaker," I may say "this is I." The answer would imply not a judgment but a correction; it would mean "this speaker is not *this* or object to myself, *this* as distinct from me is here false, the fact being I." So one may say "that snake is but a rope" where what is meant is that the snake is illusory, the rope being the fact. But the statement "I am this speaker" or "I said *I*" would not be false in such a context: it would be a mode of expressing what is called personal identity. Nevertheless it is not a judgment: my consciousness of personal identity is not a recognitive judgment as it is ordinarily taken to be. In my answer "I am this speaker," the predicate does not appear to me, as it appears to the questioner, as what the subject may not be. The pastness of the subject, moreover, as implied in the predicate—this speaker being I who *spoke*—is not consciously relative to the presentness of the subject. In saying "I spoke," I make no assertion at all about myself being *now*, the pastness of "spoke" being consciously distinguished only from the present *objective* situation. The belief in my pastness can never be formulated *by me* as the judgment "I who am now am I who was then." It is only another person who can assert my personal identity in a recognitive judgment. I cannot deny the judgment and may take it as a symbolic expression of my felt belief. My personal identity, however, is to me only a felt content which though not false is not *asserted* by me. The equation of *I* and *this* is then logically unintelligible, being the rejection of *this* in the form "this is I" and only a felt content in the form "I am this."

6. The object can be pointed out without the use of a word but it is expressible by the single word *this*. The subject cannot be indicated except by a word and the word for it is not *I* only but any personal pronoun (or any word the use of which is ultimately explained by a personal pronoun). The subject is what is intended by the words *I, you*, or *he* and though it is always what can call itself *I*, the use of *you* or *he* is as directly intelligible as the use of *I* and need not be explained by it. There is, however, a characteristic difference between the first person and the other persons. If *this* means the object, there is no occasion to consciously identify it with *I*, though I may be implicitly identified with my body.

But I am somehow conscious of an identity between another person and his body, conscious of them as distinct and yet one. The relation accordingly of *you* and *he* to *this* and *I* requires closer examination.

7. *You* and *he* are to me subjects individualized in the objective body, the body being, however, as much distinguished from them as from myself. Like their bodies they also can be spoken of as individual, but while the individuality of *he* is evidently derived from his body which is *this* to me, the individuality of *you* appears to be prior to that of your body. You are individual to me primarily through my act of addressing and only secondarily through what appears to my imagination as your identification with or appropriation of your body. *He* is individual to me only through his body being imagined as identified with or appropriated by him. *This* body is presented to me first through which I apprehend *this* subject or *he*. It may be—though it is not necessary—that before I can address you, I have to apprehend you as *this* subject or *he*; but *this* subject appears to me as *you*, only as I address. To say "this is you," is to mean, in fact, that this person is not *this* person, the third person, or *he*: it is to imply a correction as in the statement "this is I." The statement "this is he," however, implies a belief though like "I am this," it represents a felt content and not the content of a judgment. My identification of a body presented to me first with the subject *he* is not the knowledge of this object being identical with him, since the object is as much distinct from him as from me though I cannot assert his distinction from his body. I apprehend the third person as distinct from me, only as I take him to be individualized in his body. Conceived apart from his body, he would be known neither as distinct from me nor therefore as identical with me but only as one who can call himself *I*; and there would be as little occasion to say of him that he is his body as to say of me that I am my body. The statement "he is this" is thus excluded but the statement "you are this" would, like "this is he," represent a belief that is not knowledge, a felt content that is only symbolized as a judgment. The apprehension of *you*, however, logically precedes while that of *he* follows the apprehension of *this* or the body appropriated. There is no occasion to say, as has been explained, either "this is I" or "I am this," where *this* stands for my body: and where *this* means a temporal determination of myself, the

former represents a correction and the latter a felt and believed content.

8. Thus of the six possible equations of *this* with *I, you* or *he,* three are excluded and the three that are believed, namely, "I am this" (in the sense of myself as then), "you are this" (your body), and "this (his body) is he," represent a felt or imagined content that is not known. The object as meant by *this* is known as distinct from the subject as intended by a personal pronoun; and the subject may also be said to be known in itself, being what is either illusorily or imaginatively spoken of as *this* but is not known to be related to *this* either in the way of identity or distinction. The correction implied in the statement "this is I" indicates the nature of the subject such as it is aware of before it calls itself *I* and incarnates itself in the spoken word. *This* here means myself who spoke and was in the past and the correction is to the effect that the this-ness or pastness is not really mine and only illusorily appears so, that not *this I* but the unspecified *I* should be taken as the subject. There is no denial, however, of the subject being objectifiable as *this* or *then* but the objectification is an incarnation in which the projected objectivity is not known as a determination belonging to the subject, the subject being felt to be dissociated from it. The subject as *you* or *he,* so far as known, is not known as *this* or the appropriated body. You, as addressed and conceived to be logically prior to your body, are not known by me like your body as distinct from me, being only felt to be the subject that I am distinct from. So, too, if *his* body is known to be distinct from him and from me, *he,* if conceived at all apart from his body, is known not as distinct from or identical with me but as only distinct. *You* and *he* are to my knowledge as much unique as what is intended by the word *I,* being, in fact, understood simply as one who can call himself *I.* The three persons are not known to be distinct from or identical with one another.

9. The object is known as distinct from the subject but the subject is only known in itself and felt to be free or dissociated from the object. I feel dissociated from the object as I feel dissociated from the subject *you* or *he* that appears to me somehow "identified" with the object. I am aware of alienating you by the fact of addressing and of him being alienated from me as his body is alienated. I actively "dissimilate" you and, therefore, also the body that you appropriate and feel unable to "assimilate" him

and, therefore, his body with which he is found identified. The object in either case is a body somehow one with a subject which I would not or cannot identify with myself. With regard to my own body, I only do *not* feel actually dissociated from it and am not *consciously* identified with it. I am indeed individualized in my body but I am not introspectively aware of it. I am aware of myself as *this* not in the sense of my body but only in the sense of myself in a temporal position, myself as having been, for example, in the past and having spoken of myself as *I*. *This* is here only thought and not known as distinct from myself and I am conscious not only of being dissociated from it but also of its distinction from myself being illusory. Thus everywhere the subject is known in itself and not as related to the object, being at best felt to be dissociated from the object with which it was identified.

10. The subject, understood as the unique speaker—actual or possible—of the word *I*, and the object that is meant as distinct from the subject are the two things that are known. The reality of what is meant can always be doubted and so the object is not known with the same assurance as the subject that cannot be said to be meant. There may be such a thing as an illusory object; and in the statement "this is I," as already explained, *this* is understood as an objectivity that is annulled. The idea of a possible annulment of objectivity being there, an object that is given as distinct from the subject can be conceived to be not distinct, though the distinction may not be actually cancelled. The denial of reality is intelligible only about what is meant, the negation of the meant being also either actually or problematically meant. The unreality, however, of the subject as intended but not meant by *I* is meaningless. It is not only inconceivable like the opposite of an axiom; it is not even tried to be conceived, a content being taken to be inconceivable only after it has been tried to be conceived. The word *I* expresses a unique and unanalyzable content from which all that is meant is distinct and which yet is understood and unquestioningly believed. The belief cannot be called a grammatical superstition, though the fact believed is inexpressible except in language by a grammatical pronoun. The subject appears as a known fact, only as it is spoken of through a personal pronoun or conceived to be so speakable. One's private awareness of *I* before its expression in speech is indeed knowledge but the *I* here does not appear as a known fact distinct from the

knower. To be aware of the subject as a known fact is to be aware of it as a spoken fact. It is not so about the object of which one may be aware as known even if unnamed. The subject as spoken fact is, however, a meant fact.

11. The metaphysical controversy about the reality of the subject is only about the subject viewed in some sense as object. The thinnest sense in which it is objectified is "being taken as meant." Ordinarily the validity of this degree of objectification of the subject is not questioned, nor therefore the possibility of a dispute about its reality. If, however, the subject is taken, as explained, to be what is expressed by the word *I* as expressing itself, it is not meant or at best meant as unmeant and is accordingly above metaphysical dispute. There is properly no metaphysic of the subject, if by metaphysic is understood an enquiry into the reality conceived as meanable. Even the unknowable thing-in-itself of Spencer and Kant is not taken to be unmeanable. It is at worst taken to be a problem in meaning. The knowable is meant and the negation of the knowable is, if not meant, tried to be meant, being not a gratuitous combination of words but a believed content that is problematically formulated. The subject which is also believed is formulated as *I* which is, however, understood as unmeanable though not as a mere word like *abracadabra*. The understanding here is not a mystic intuition though it may point to its possibility, nor the intuition of a meaning that can be a term of a judgment, nor yet the thought of a meaning that is not known because not intuited or that is known without being intuited. It is somewhere midway between a mystic intuition and the consciousness of a meaning, being the believing awareness of a speakable content, the negation of which is unmeaning and which, therefore, is not a meaning. What is claimed to be mystically intuited is speakable only in metaphor which presents a contradiction in meaning and what is affirmed or denied in metaphysic is a meanable. The subject as I is neither contradictory nor meanable and the exposition of it accordingly is intermediate between mysticism and metaphysic. As, however, the subject is communicable by speech without metaphor, it cannot be taken as falling outside philosophical enquiry.

12. The attitude of metaphysics like that of the sciences including psychology is objective. It seeks to know reality as distinct from the knowing of it, as objective, at least, in the sense of being

meant. Knowing as a fact from which the known is distinct is not properly the subject either of psychology or of metaphysics. Psychological introspection is at best awareness of the *knownness* of the object, the knownness being meant as an accident of the object, as an abstraction from the known object, as the difference between the object as known and the object that is only believed, or as the object *coming* to be known. If there be a metaphysic of the psychological fact of knownness, its problem would be to determine what it is in the object that makes it known and not what the subject should be in order that it may know. Knowing from which all that is known or objective is distinct is dealt with in epistemology which distinguishes it as a function from the object but does not, therefore, take it to be a known fact. Knowing is not given as distinct to introspection nor inferred as distinct, being only distinct through the self-conscious act of distinguishing it. Knowing cannot be known as a fact unless the distinguishing of knowing be the knowing itself, unless, in fact, the distinctness of knowing from the distinguishing of it appears illusory, even as *this* appears illusory in the apparent judgment "this is I." To realize that the distinctness of knowing is entirely through the distinguishing of it is to realize knowing as a self-evidencing fact, as not distinct from the object known but as unrelated or illusorily related to it, as not the knowing *of* object but as the solitary fact of the subject itself. Knowing is not thus known in epistemology which, however, does not disbelieve in its facthood. Were it known as a meanable fact, there would be room for the metaphysical inference of the subject as the ground of it. As it is, knowing is only symbolized as an activity; and the inference of the subject as the agent is rightly characterized as involving a grammatical superstition. There is no room for metaphysics after epistemology has worked itself out of the objective attitude of metaphysics and the sciences by distinguishing knowing from the object known.

13. At the same time the belief in the facthood of knowing is there, as epistemology is not an enquiry into the significance of the mere phrase "knowing *of* object." The belief is in the facthood of the knowing function, function being a metaphor for a positive something which is literally expressed only in the negative way as what the known object is not and being thus not even an accomplished meaning. The awareness of this unmeant some-

thing involves, however, a higher certitude than the belief in the meant object. Epistemology claims this certitude though it cannot justify it and has to recognize it to be other than the certitude of knowledge. Thus it appears that while the subject can be said to be known by itself and the meant object to be known as distinct from the subject, a subjective function like knowing is only believed though it may be with greater assurance than the object. The knowing of an object is not given as distinct from the object and *is* only in being distinguished from it, as relating and not as related to it, as not distinct from the distinguishing but not therefore as identical with it, as the free reference of the subject to the object. The subject is, as explained before, free from the object in the sense of being known by itself and not as related to it either in the way of identity or distinction. The knowing function represents a positive mode of this freedom, the freedom of the subject to relate to object without getting related to it, which is believed to be more certain than the object but is not known. We are aware of knowing a content when it is formulated and believed to be independent of our formulating, speaking, or distinguishing act. It is so believed when it is felt either to be a given distinct—as in the case of the object known—or to be "incarnated" in the formulation, in the sense explained, of being expressed as expressing or self-revealing—as in the case of the subject. Subjective function or the positive freedom of the subject to refer to the object is felt to be neither and is accordingly said to be only believed. The belief is bound up with the knowledge of the self-evidencing subject and as belief in a content which is like the subject itself not presented as meant, it is incapable of being doubted and is more certain than the knowledge of a meant object.

14. The three believed contents—the subject, the positive freedom of the subject, and the meant object—are all speakable and it is from the speakable that we have to start in philosophy. The subject is taken to be known, as one who says *I* is immediately understood by the hearer through the word but not as meant by the word. The speaker is understood as revealing himself to another of whom he is positively aware as distinct but not as independent of his distinguishing. The positive awareness may be called feeling of alienating the subject *you*. What is known is the body of the other subject as an object distinct from the speaker. The speaking subject may thus be said to have a feeling

of relating itself to the object, of addressing itself to it as though it were *you*. This felt relating is the positive freedom of the subject having different felt modes like knowing, feeling, or being which though not objectively meanable can be symbolized by objective meanings. Such symbolic elaboration of the felt or believed spiritual functions would be a procedure of philosophy intermediate between the recognition of the subject purely through the intention of the word *I* and the inferential inquiry into the reality behind the meant object which is called metaphysics.

15. There is properly no metaphysic of the subject and the apparent problems about the existence of the subject and its relation to the object are really illegitimate. The question if the subject is real is unmeaning, for the subject as I is not a meaning. The reality of the subject is known in the direct understanding of the word *I* as used by a speaker, which is neither the understanding of its meaning nor a mystic intuition of an unspeakable content. There can be also no relation of subject to object if the subject is not objectively meant, the subject being only aware of its function of *relating* or referring to object. The subject may believe itself and the object without speaking of them but it believes its relating function only as it speaks of it. If it speaks of the object, it believes in it as meant and if it speaks of itself as I, it believes in it as unmeant. But in speaking of its function it believes in it neither as meant nor as unmeant but as being constructed as fact by being spoken. A believed content that is spoken appears objective but while the appearance is denied of the spoken subject and asserted of the spoken object, it is only not denied of the spoken function. The speaking creation of a system of subjective functions or the symbolizing elaboration of the positive freedom of the subject constitutes a special study which as not asserting meanable and justifiable truth cannot be called metaphysic and as yet inviting to believe and exhibiting the interval between the self-evidencing I and objectively knowable truth has to be taken as coming within philosophy.

16. There is no theoretic passage from what is meanable or objectively knowable to the subjectively knowable I; metaphysics cannot pass out of the region of meanings. Epistemology indeed deals with the subjective function behind the accomplished meaning but it does not assert it as fact. It *assumes* the facthood of the function—knowing *of* object—and only paraphrases the intention of the preposition *of* in reference to the different modes of

knownness of the object such as are presented in psychology. The facthood of the knowing function and of subjective function in general is believed though not known and is elaborated into a system of symbolisms in a new philosophical study which may be called Spiritual or Transcendental psychology. The symbolism is fact in the sense of being the form of the non-theoretic or spiritually practical mode of escaping the objective knowing attitude of which the meaning attitude represents the subtlest stage. No meanable truth is self-evidencing, its negation being at least a problem in meaning and yet the self-evidencing I is the type of truth. The implication is that meanable truth which cannot be denied to be truth has to be realized as self-evidencing, not by being objectively thought again but by the spiritual cultivation of a subjective attitude. As the positive freedom of relating—which is an objective attitude—is to the objectively meant relation, so is the negative freedom in the cultivation of the subjective attitude to the positive freedom of the objective attitude. Spiritual psychology symbolizes the subjective attitude by the objective attitude from which it seeks to be freed. The modes of subjectivity are the modes of freeing oneself from the modes of objectivity.

17. Hence comes the justification of the name Spiritual *psychology*. Psychology, as has been pointed out, deals not properly with knowing but with knownness as a character or aspect of the object. It deals, as we may say generally, not with subjective function but with the object regarded explicitly as distinct from it, as known, felt, or willed. If there be a metaphysic of psychology, its problem would be what there is in the object to make it known, felt, or willed. We are aware of an object that was only believed as coming to be known though its existence is not asserted or denied before the knowing. The metaphysical problem about the objective knownness, feltness, and so forth, is intelligible though it may not be capable of objective solution. The distinguishing of knownness, et cetera, as an abstraction from the object, as the objectivity of the object is what is called psychological introspection. The distinguishing of the subjective function of knowing, et cetera, as other than this abstraction of objectivity may also be called introspection and, it may be, with greater right. If psychological introspection be an abstracting from the object, this introspection is a creative symbolizing, the functions being subjective facts and not mere abstractions, though they are only believed and not known. The symbolizing of the subjective func-

tion is by a mode of objectivity like knownness, dissociation from which is precisely indicated by the word function. Thus the functions represent the modes of freedom from the corresponding psychological abstractions. The consciousness of freedom is as direct as that of such abstraction and its content can only be indicated as some sort of negation of the abstraction. If the consciousness of the abstraction be called psychological introspection, the consciousness of freedom may be called spiritual introspection and the philosophical study that is based on it may be designated Spiritual psychology.

18. The metaphysical problem—what it is in the object that determines its known or felt appearance—assumes that an appearance of object that is not unreal is caused by object, which implies further that object has an assured reality independent of the subject. It has, however, been indicated that the reality of object is not incapable of being doubted like the reality of the subject; and even if object be as real as the subjective process that refers to it, it is not necessary that its relatedness to the subject should be caused at all. The emergence of such relatedness of an object is an event in time, only so far as it is not other than the emergence of the object or of an objective situation comprising it. The knownness or feltness of an object is an abstraction, the problem of the causation of which is illegitimate. Change in the object, as distinguished from the object, is also an abstraction but it is still understood as objective fact though unseparated from the object. Knownness, et cetera, or the objectivity of the object is an abstraction that has no objective meaning at all by itself and about which, therefore, the demand for causal explanation is meaningless. The explanation of the emergence of the object *as related* to the subject is an ordinary objective or scientific problem and no separate explanation can be demanded for the emergence of the abstraction of relatedness. The metaphysical problem is thus apparently only a problem in meaning—how relatedness to the subject can be spoken of as a character of the object.

19. Spiritual psychology, however, has a place because its business is not to explain or to solve a problem. Its business is in the first place to interpret empirical psychology in terms of the positively felt and believed freedom of the subject from objectivity; and next to elaborate modes of freedom that have no reference to object at all, to conceive the possible illusoriness of all objects and thus to assign an intelligible place to what is ordinar-

ily scouted as spiritual mysticism. In the objective attitude, the knownness or feltness of the object appears positive and knowing or feeling appears as its problematic negation. In the subjective attitude, the case is reversed: freedom is positively believed and the relatedness of the object to the subject—its objectivity—appears as constructed, as not belonging to the object in the sense change belongs to it and is thus understood as the self-negation or alienated shadow of the subject. In the objective attitude again, *this* or object appears to exist beyond its *this-ness* or relatedness to the subject, while in the subjective attitude not only is the transcendent *this* rejected as meaningless, *this-ness* —meaning the so-called psychological entities, knownness or feltness —appears also not to be *given* as distinct to introspection but to exist only as distinguished or constructed, this distinguishing or constructing being felt as less certain than the self-evident subject behind it. The object or *this* beyond objectivity, *this-ness* or relatedness to subject is sought to be known not only in the metaphysic of psychology, but in all metaphysic. From the standpoint of spiritual psychology, this transcendent object is simply meaningless and metaphysic is the quest of a chimera. All so-called metaphysical problems are to it symbolisms for modes of freedom, the forms of spiritual discipline by which the objective attitude has to be renounced and the positive subjective functioning has to be reversed in direction toward the realization of the subject behind it.

20. Kant's critical philosophy may be taken as a disguised form of spiritual psychology as thus conceived. The elaboration of the three modes of belief—theoretic, practical, and aesthetic—is transcendental psychology, the spiritual equivalent offered by him for dogmatic metaphysics. The start is from epistemology which assumes the reality of the subject and subjective function though it does not explicitly confess in the case of the knowing function that it is only assumed or believed to be real and presents instead a make-believe of inference in the so-called transcendental deductions. The other functions are, however, definitely asserted to be only believed: the reality of the willing function, for example, is taken to be apprehended in the willing consciousness only. The confession is not made about the knowing function because epistemology is to Kant not so much a branch of transcendental psychology as a prolegomena to it, concerned not with the presentation of subjective fact but with the meaning of

the preposition *of* in "knowledge of object," the facthood of which is implicitly taken for granted. Its interest is still in the object, in the knownness or objectivity of the object which it seeks to understand theoretically as knowing. It does not abandon the objective procedure of metaphysics and the sciences, even though it sets itself to correct the conceit of independent objectivity. The objective procedure may be necessary to show up the seamy character of objectivity and may also imply the truthful admission that we do not get rid of our actual belief in the independent object by the mere thinking criticism of it. But it misleads so far as it presents the function as an objective meaning and does not recognize that it is believed without being meant. Epistemology might be mistaken as only a philological study, unless it is consciously viewed as rooted in the faith in the facthood of the knowing function and unless the so-called deduction that it presents is definitely known to be not inferential and not literally meant but to be the mere symbolization by logical form of what is immediately believed as spiritual fact.

21. The persisting objective attitude of Kant in his first critique explains not only his admission of the thing-in-itself and his denial of self-knowledge but also his disbelief in the possibility of a spiritual discipline of the theoretic reason through which self-knowledge may be attainable. From the subjective standpoint, object beyond knownness, *this* beyond *this-ness* is, as explained, meaningless. It may be that, wedded as we are to our body, we cannot get rid of the objective attitude and the tendency to look beyond the constructed object to the purely given. But not to be able to deny need not imply admission and though the Kantian disclaimer of idealism as accomplished knowledge is intelligible, his admission of the unknowable reality appears to be an unwarrantable surrender to realism. After the resolution of the objectivity of the object into the knowing function, the independence of the object becomes inconceivable though it continues to be believed. Such a belief cannot be asserted though it cannot also be rejected. Realism should, therefore, be held as suspect though idealism is only a faith and not knowledge. But the faith has to be cherished and there should be a subjective discipline to get rid of the persisting realistic belief. Kant does not admit such a discipline at least for the theoretic reason.

22. Self-knowledge is denied by Kant: the self cannot be known but only thought through the objective categories—unity, substantiality, et cetera, there being no intuition of it. The view presented so far is that the subject is known though neither thought (meant) nor intuited. It is known as what the speaker of *I* is understood to intend by it. The understanding is a direct believing in something that is not meant but revealed as revealing itself, a question about the reality of which does not arise and is unmeaning. The subject is thus known by itself, as not meant but speakable and not as either related or relating to the object. It is, however, believed as relating to object and symbolized as such by the objective relations. The modes of relating are at the same time the modes of freeing from objectivity, the forms of the spiritual discipline by which, it may be conceived, the outgoing reference to the object is turned backwards and the immediate knowledge of the *I* as content is realized in an ecstatic intuition.

23. Spiritual progress means the realization of the subject as free. The realization may or may not involve a specific activity of the subject. There are those to whom it is only a resultant experience. One lives an objectively good or full life and finds his self correspondingly realized. Others, however, recognize a specific discipline or consecutive method of activity for such realization. The consciousness of perfection, freedom, or salvation as the end is to them a demand for some kind of activity of the subject toward itself. This cult of the subject, as it might be called, takes various forms but they all involve a feeling of dissociation of the subject from the object, an awareness of the subject as what the object is not. The specific activity demanded is primarily in the inwardizing direction and secondarily, if at all, in the direction of creating objective or social values. One demand among others—all being absolute demands—is that the subjective function being essentially the knowing of the object as distinct from it, this knowing which is only believed and not known as fact *has* to be known as fact, as the self-evidencing reality of the subject itself. This would be the cult of the subject *par excellence*, a spiritual discipline of the theoretic reason, a method of cognitive inwardizing, the possibility of which, as indeed of any method of realization, is not ordinarily recognized.

24. The possibility of such a method has to be exhibited in Spiritual psychology. A method implies a series of consecutive

steps for the realization of an end. The steps in this case should correspond to a gradation of subjective functions, of modes of freedom from the object. Identified as we are with our body, our freedom from the perceived object is actually realized only in our bodily consciousness, though even this, as will appear later, is only imperfectly realized. Bodily consciousness may as well be called conscious body, there being no dissociation at this stage of the subject from the body, though the extra-organic object is known to be distinct from it. The next stage of freedom is suggested by the distinction of the perceived object including the body from the ghostly object in the form of the image, idea, and meaning which may be all designated "presentation." Consciousness as undissociated from such presentation, but dissociated from the perceived and felt body, may be called presentational or psychic subjectivity. The dissociation of the subject or consciousness from this presentation conceived as a kind of object would be the next stage of freedom which may be called non-presentational or spiritual subjectivity. The three broad stages of subjectivity would then be the bodily, the psychical, and the spiritual and each would comprise substages. Wedded as we are to our body, actual freedom is felt only in bodily subjectivity and freedom in the higher stages as suggested by psychology is believed not as what is actual but as what has to be achieved or realized. The grades of subjectivity imply grades of objectivity, the terms being conceived in a relative sense. To spiritual subjectivity, the psychical is objective, and so to psychic subjectivity the bodily, and to bodily subjectivity, the extra-organic is objective. The objective at any stage is known as distinct from the subjective next to it, which, however, is not known as distinct from the objective but only felt and believed to be free or dissociated from it. The elaboration of these stages of freedom in spiritual psychology would suggest the possibility of a consecutive method of realizing the subject as absolute freedom, of retracting the felt positive freedom toward the object into pure intuition of the self.

Chapter 2
Psychic Fact

25. The facts of empirical psychology have to be interpreted from the subjective standpoint in spiritual psychology. What is called psychological introspection is apparently a process of abstraction from the object of its modes of relatedness to the subject. This relatedness, viewed as a character of the object, is the so-called psychic fact. There is a difference, however, between this objective character and other objective characters. A character of a thing is an abstraction distinguished from it but not imaginable as separated from it. As distinct *in* the thing, it is a fact; but as spoken of by itself, it need not mean a fact. An abstraction like color, for example, means a fact while an abstraction like intensity does not mean a fact though the intensity of color as in the color is a fact. These two kinds of abstraction may be designated respectively as of the first degree and of the second degree. Knownness or any other mode of relatedness of object to subject, as taken by itself, is an abstraction of the second degree: it does not mean a fact though the object as thus related is a fact. There is a difference, again, between this relatedness and intensity as abstractions. In the knowing of a bright color, color is not known as distinct from brightness, being only spoken of as distinct while in

the knowing of the knownness of an object, the object—at least as non-perceptually known—is known as distinct from its knownness or presentation. Knownness or relatedness is a floating adjective of the object like its beauty or like the absence of an object as a character of the object in which it is absent. The so-called psychic fact, as abstracted from the object by psychological introspection, may thus be taken as a floating abstraction of the second degree. It is interpreted from the subjective standpoint in spiritual psychology as a subjective function that is a fact.

26. To psychological introspection with its objective attitude, psychic fact is a character of the object, existing like the object even apart from introspection. It is, however, only quasi-objective: unlike the object which when not perceived is known to exist in some other mode of cognition, psychic fact that is believed during introspection to exist is believed on the testimony of the same introspection to exist also apart from it. The perception of an object is immersed in the object and as such is not, as will appear later, knowable in *direct* introspection. As the object is only indirectly known to be distinct from the perception of it, perception cannot be taken as a given psychic fact for purposes of psychology. Feeling, again, is a psychic fact only as the feltness of a known object and as bound up with its knownness; and if there is feeling not bound up with object-cognition, it cannot appear to introspection to exist apart from it and as such cannot be called psychic fact. To start with at any rate then, the term *psychic* has to be restricted to modes of subjectivity that lie between sense-perception on the one hand and such objectless feeling on the other.

27. Psychic fact is either the knownness of object or the feltness, et cetera, of known object, being fact from which object is distinguishable. What does not involve the knowledge of object is no psychic fact. Is mere imagination then—imagination of the *imaginary* which is no known object—to be regarded as psychic fact? What is imagined need not be imaginary and even what is taken as imaginary is not wholly imaginary. The imagination of a golden mountain involves not only the awareness of what never is but also the belief in the possibility of a mountain being made of gold, in the compatibility of the objective facts, *golden* and *mountain*. This compatibility is not imaginary, is not merely an imagined relation of two images but is an objective fact expressed in an abstract and periphrastic way. The imagination of golden

mountain is a psychic fact so far as it implies an unrejected belief in such objective fact.

28. But is the awareness of the content as what never is, to be taken as psychic fact? The belief in the absence of what is at some time somewhere is still knowledge of objective fact. Even the awareness of what never is, where there was wrong belief in it or a real question about it, implies an unrejected belief in some objective fact. But golden mountain is imaginary in the sense that it not only never is but that it does not even suggest a real question about its existence. The awareness of such an imaginary content implies the rejection of all belief in objective fact. Introspection is belief in the psychic fact of believing in an objective fact. Is there a belief in the absence of objective belief or, in other words, introspection into the consciousness of the imaginary? There may only be disbelief or no-belief in believing and so there seems to be no introspection into *mere* imaging, the awareness of it being other than, though on a level with, introspection. What introspection does not reveal is no psychic fact and hence the consciousness of the imaginary is no psychic fact.

29. Is there such a thing as objectless feeling, feeling that does not involve knowledge of an objective fact? The feeling that we introspectively believe as being a fact outside introspection is the feeling of an object as known, from which indeed the knowledge is distinguished but which is not itself distinguished from the knowledge. Objectless feeling, if such there be, would be like introspection itself only a non-psychic fringe of some psychic fact. The general possibility of such feeling will be exhibited later but it may be asked at this stage if the feeling of an object that is believed to be illusory should be taken as psychic fact. The past belief in the snake, for example, which is now known to be only a rope, was bound up with a feeling of fear. Is the fear now believed as a past psychic fact? Obviously, we do not believe it now as the fear of *that* snake. But it may be said that although *that* snake is not believed, the characteristic feeling of bodily reaction in the past is believed, which is just the past fear of the snake. A feeling, however, is essentially individual and its individuality is constituted by the belief in the individuality of its object. The reduction of what was taken to be the fear of snake to the feeling of bodily reaction would be the disbelief in *that* feeling. Belief in the past fear of some object, indeed, remains over with the belief in the past bodily condition. But it remains over only in the sense of not being rejected and not of being asserted, and it remains over not

by itself but as only the non-psychic fringe of the memory of the past bodily condition.

30. When we speak of the feeling of an object, we are not introspectively aware of the feeling as distinct from and accompanying the belief in the object. We do not distinguish the feeling at all from the belief though we may be aware of the belief without the feeling. The feeling, in fact, refers to the object as directly as the belief and along with it. It is artificial to understand it to refer to the object in the first instance related to the belief in the object and, therefore, to take the fear of the snake now believed to be illusory as fear related to the past belief in snake as distinct from the snake. We cannot say that the fear of the snake was just as real as the past belief in the snake. The false belief, now that it is corrected, is known to have been a fact, for the correction can be expressed in the form "what *was believed* to be snake was not snake but rope." It cannot be said, however, about the fear that it was fear of the rope or of *that* snake or of that idea of snake or that it was fear of nothing at all. The rope was the cause but not the object of the past feeling; so, too, was the idea of the snake while *that* snake cannot be called its object because it is now disbelieved. Nor can we take the object to have been snake-in-general, for fear of such a generality is, at best, a disposition to feel and not an actual feeling. We believe, indeed, in the past feeling of a characteristic bodily reaction but a bodily feeling is not the consciousness of the body as its object, there being as little conscious distinction between bodily feeling and felt body as between perception and perceived object, while the past feeling in this case was distinctly consciousness of something as object. We cannot say that the fear was of nothing at all, since we do not remember the feeling as unformulated. After the belief in the snake has been corrected, it is impossible to describe as past *fact* what was called fear of the snake when it was believed. It may be arbitrary to deny that the fear was a fact but it cannot be asserted to have been fact because its object is now indescribable. The feeling then of an object now believed to be illusory cannot, at least, be asserted to have been a psychic fact.

31. A psychic fact involves belief in an objective fact and introspection into it is a belief in such belief. The awareness of the imaginary as such, being a disbelief in objective belief, has been shown to be other than but on a level with introspection. Are these modes of subjectivity to be taken as psychic facts? A psychic

fact may involve belief in another psychic fact but it is primarily a belief in some objective fact. One may remember, for example, an objective event and also be aware of the subjective fact of its having been previously known. Such awareness is not memory unless the past knowing of the event was itself known in the past and should be taken accordingly as nothing but introspection. It is no psychic fact by itself but is only the transitive fringe of the substantive fact of objective memory. Introspection is always awareness of a psychic fact that is past though the psychic fact need not be known as past as in this case and may persist at the time of introspection. In any case introspection into it is bound up with another psychic fact like memory as in this case, which is primarily a belief in the object and need not have this fringe. Like introspection which is belief in believing, disbelief in believing also—the consciousness of the imaginary, which is not introspection but may be taken as coordinate with it—is a non-psychic fringe of a substantive psychic fact. The correction of an objective illusion appears to present a difficulty, since in it we are aware not of the past object but of the past belief in object, the awareness being also introspection. It implies, however, a present disbelief in the object which as implying in every case an unrejected belief in something objective is psychic fact and the introspective belief in the past fact of belief is the non-psychic fringe of this psychic fact.

32. So then we conclude that a form of consciousness which does not involve belief in an objective fact is no psychic fact but is only the fringe of some psychic fact that involves such belief and need not have the fringe. The fringe may epistemologically be primary or secondary in respect of the psychic fact but never stands by itself. Introspection, for example, is primary in respect of the psychic fact of which it is a fringe while the awareness of an illusory object is secondary in respect of the belief that remains over after the correction. Again, the individual feeling that cannot be denied as bound up with the past belief in the object that is now taken to be illusory is primary in respect of the remembered body-feeling and may be taken as secondary in respect of the present remembering of the bodily feeling.

33. A psychic fact is or involves not merely the belief in an objective fact but the knowledge of it. We are aware of a belief as

having been belief in an object as now formulated if the object is now either known or disbelieved. It is in introspection into knowledge or in the consciousness of the unreal object as such that we realize that we believed before we knew or disbelieved and that there was then no awareness of a distinction of the object believed from the belief. Knowledge as distinct from mere belief involves awareness of the distinction, this being testified by introspection into knowledge even about such knowledge as precedes introspection. The distinction that is presented to introspection is believed to exist also apart from introspection. The distinction of the object from the belief in it is something more than the object itself, though it cannot be said to be not objective. It is just what is called presentation of the object, which is taken as a psychic fact only as it is in introspection abstracted from the object. Presentation and object are so related that while the latter is given distinct from the former, the former is not given distinct from the latter, being only abstracted or tried to be distinguished in introspection.

34. Two extreme cases have to be considered in understanding this relation of presentation and object. In perceptual knowledge, the object does not appear distinct from its presentation; and in perceptual illusion, there is apparently the presentation only, with no object distinct from it. We do not, indeed, introspectively distinguish perceptual knowledge from its object but still such knowledge is not mere belief inasmuch as in it the object is given as distinct in itself though not from its presentation and has not to be distinguished, as in the case of mere belief, in a later act of knowledge. The object explicitly appears distinct from its presentation in non-perceptual knowledge, such distinction being the condition of possible introspection into it. There is accordingly no introspection into perceptual knowledge, though other knowledge, when introspected into, may be distinguished from perceptual knowledge. Still the perceived object being consciously distinct in itself may *be* distinct from its presentation, though it is not consciously so appreciated. Knowledge involves only the conscious or evident distinctness of the believed object, whether or not there is the consciousness of the presentation as that from which it is distinct.

35. Perceptual illusion presents another kind of difficulty. The perceived object being disbelieved is not removed altogether from consciousness. The appearance may be still presented though such presentation would not embody belief in an object. Like mere imagination, mere perceptual presentation is no psychic fact at all to which object may be related in the way of distinction: the awareness of it is only the fringe of perception as a fact. In the correction of an illusion as expressed in "not snake but rope," the rope is utterly unrelated to the mere presentation: the word *not* in it means rejection only and no distinction, the rejection being the fringe of the present perception of rope. The awareness of the mere presentation is not belief in it, though unlike mere imagination the presentation is not explicitly disbelieved. The mere presentation as this equivocal something that is neither believed nor disbelieved is very different from the presentation from which the object is said to be distinct in knowledge and which is definitely believed in introspection and taken to embody belief in an object. It should, in fact, be designated by some word other than presentation.

36. Intermediate between perceptual knowledge and perceptual illusion are the other forms of knowledge involving a conscious distinction of the known object from its presentation. It is in the awareness of the illusory that the presentation definitely emerges from the perceived object into which it was merged. But this emergence or freedom is also the death of the presentation in the sense that it no longer embodies belief. The presentation is a fact to introspection so long as the object presented is believed and distinguished from it. Introspection into non-perceptual knowledge is thus a belief in presentation. As introspection is the belief that its content is a fact even apart from introspection, the presentation is a fact, the facthood of which consists in its being a belief in a distinct objective fact. As there is no direct introspection into perceptual knowledge, there is no consciousness here, but not therefore a denial, of a presentation from which the object is distinct. Introspection into non-perceptual knowledge is such consciousness of presentation of object from which object is distinct.

37. The distinctness of the object from its presentation does not

mean the distinctness of the presentation from its object. The introspective belief in the presentation is belief in the object as well and so presentation is not not-objective, not illusory nor purely subjective. As the object, however, is distinguished from it in non-perceptual knowledge, it is the perceivable object and something more that is believed in, something that is not known but is wanted to be known. The knowledge of the distinction of the object as imagined to be perceived from the presentation is the belief embodied in presentation in something that cannot be imagined to be perceived but appears still as adjectival to the perceivable object. This believed something is, if known, known as unknown and as only wanted to be known.

38. There are different grades of non-perceptual knowledge implying different modes of presentation or belief in object. By "perception" is meant here external perception of object. What is the knowledge of the body from within, body as internally felt and not externally observed? The observed object including the observed body is distinguished from the internally felt body which thus is no part of the observable world and yet is believed not as other than the observed body but as its character of internality. Again, there is the immediate apprehension of the absence of an object which cannot be said to be known by external perception, at least, in the ordinary sense and yet is known as a present objective fact. There is memory which is belief in the perceivable object as past, pastness being an unperceivable character of the object. Imagination so far as it involves belief is non-perceptual apprehension of the object as forming or becoming formed to be a perceptible object. Inference, again, is belief in the perceivable object as involving the unperceivable character of necessity. None of these non-perceptual forms of apprehension is mere belief; the object cannot be said to be not known in them and yet each is a belief in something that cannot be known by external perception and, being still about the object and indefinite, is wanted to be somehow known or realized. Perceptual knowledge is the actual standard of knowledge. The other modes of apprehension imply it, are not taken in introspection to be mere belief, and involve further a belief in something not yet

known but which may be known in some ideal mode of realization or intuition.

39. Perception as the actual standard of knowledge not only lends the cognitive character to the other modes of apprehension but also prevents them from reaching their ideal completion. The internality of the felt body, absence or pastness, forming or necessity as facts are wanted to be known as the object is actually known in perception. Yet these are facts of such a kind that if they were so known, the perception of the object could not remain unaffected in its cognitive character. So far as these modes of apprehension are knowledge, they are knowledge of these facts as adjectival characters of the perceptually knowable object. These facts however, as shown about the general character of knownness, are floating adjectives from which the objects, to which they are ascribed are distinct, though as abstractions of the second degree, they have to be referred adjectivally to the object as substantive. They are, however, necessarily symbolized as substantive by objective metaphors, being not merely thought but sought to be believed as though they were substantive objects. If they could be known as such, the actual perceived object would be, at best, a particular manifestation of a more essential object. They are, however, not known as substantive and there is only the metaphysical *aspiration* to extend and deepen the conception of the object. They are not known because as a matter of fact, though not necessarily, we are wedded to the body and to the perceptual object that is organic to it. The identification with the object is so deep-rooted that, though not necessary, it is not annulled by any logic and may be regarded for all ordinary purposes as a "permanent illusion."

40. The believed object as perceived or imagined to be perceived is distinct from presentation but the presentation is not distinct from its object. In perceptual knowledge, if the object is not consciously distinct from its presentation, its distinction is yet knowable through some ordinary non-perceptual mode of knowledge. But if the presentation is not known as distinct from the object, it does not come to be known as such by any logic or in any ordinary form of knowledge. It is believed and symbolized as

what should be distinct: the distinction here, not being a character of the object, cannot exist unconsciously. It can exist only in being achieved or realized subjectively. The psychic fact, being essentially presentation as embodying belief, is on the one hand not imaginary or non-factual and on the other not accomplished as fact but only to be accomplished. It is at once known and unknown, its facthood being what has begun to be achieved and is yet to be completed. Introspection is belief in the psychic, not as utterly unknown but as only not isolated or freed from objective fact. The complete knowledge and facthood of the psychic has to be achieved by such isolation but the demand itself is roused by such knowledge as has already begun.

41. Psychic fact involves knowledge of object and such knowledge exists outside introspection as presentation from which object is distinct but which is not distinct from the object. Presentation is the object and more than the object, embodying, as it does, belief in something that can never be perceived by sense, from which the perceived object is distinct but which yet appears as a character of the object. As such, this presentation may be said to be known as unknown and as to be known and has to be symbolized as object, including, as it does, the object as its manifestation or appearance in some sense. Psychic fact accordingly is that of which the facthood is at once accomplished and to be accomplished, unlike the facthood of objective fact which is only accomplished and the reality like that claimed for the moral *ought* which is only to be accomplished.

42. The complete accomplishment of psychic facthood is conceivable as implying presentation that is wholly turned into known object, which would mean, not the lapse of the conscious distinction of object from presentation such as characterizes sense-perception, but the conscious or evident objectivity of what in presentation is more than the sense-given object and suggests a metaphysical reality—what in ordinary psychic fact is only not denied as objective and may be conceived to be subjective. The image of a believed object, for example, is more than the perceivable object in the sense that it appears *being* formed and not given as formed. The forming is presented as a process of the object itself and yet somehow prior to its existence as formed.

There is no ground to take it as merely subjective, for it appears to be seen in the non-introspective attitude though the object as formed is distinct from it. As a becoming of the object prior to its accomplished being, it implies a metaphysical fact that is not known as intelligibly related to the object, appearing as it does as an un-objective character of the object which is a contradiction. It is in this sense known as unknown in the object and felt as dissociated from it. If imagination were to be realized, this contradiction would disappear, the becoming would be evident as a substantive fact and the object would be seen as its contingent manifestation. The image would then be dissociated in knowledge and not in mere feeling from the object and would be said to have achieved a free existence. Similar suggestions of metaphysical reality and the possibility of realizing it would be presented by psychic states higher than the imagination.

43. To such a view a Kantian may be supposed to object that the metaphysical reality thus adumbrated in the presentation is only subjective though it appears real in the object by illusion, by a permanent illusion which we can critically correct without being able to remove. The critical correction may only be sought to be strengthened in a non-cognitive way—the moral or aesthetic way—with the entertainment of the metaphysical reality in faith. Our contention would be that the appearance of its objectivity is incomplete but not illusory; that the illusion is to take it as known but not as knowable; that if it were unknowable, it could not be entertained in faith even for non-cognitive realization and that the demand to know it is legitimate if not necessary. The thought of the metaphysical entity is a conscious problem but the problem is soluble in a mode of knowledge in which the object would appear as its free efflux, as what it can be but need not be. The metaphysical would appear in such knowledge as an evident real, as the existent fact of knowledge itself, with the object as its free possibility and as negated in its actuality.

44. That metaphysical reality is subjective is admitted in the sense that it is not an *object* behind the perceivable object. The objective attitude of metaphysics should terminate with the recognition of something that is known as unknown in the object, of the contradiction in the presented unobjective character of the

object. But this unknown something that is known as such and formulated is not *merely* subjective in the sense of being illusory or in the sense of being the content of a faith that can never be turned into knowledge. To take it as merely subjective is to assume the object to be alone knowable and to be incapable of being *known* as put forth subjectively or freely. It is to deny the facthood of the constructive function by which the perceivable object comes to be for the subject. The epistemological functions are indeed believed and not known but they are not believed as merely subjective. They are, no doubt, symbolized by objective metaphors but the symbolism is necessary and has to be entertained in faith. The demand to entertain the objective symbolism in faith is inconsistent with the *denial* of the knowability or objectivity of the functions. To be aware of a description as metaphorical but necessarily so is to take it to be unknown in the sense of being unrealized, of being imagined to be known but not yet known. It implies the possibility of knowing not indeed by any logical procedure but by a specific self-realizing activity of the imagination itself. It argues a gratuitous diffidence to take such activity to be a mystic chimera. The imagination of knowing or the symbolizing faith would not be faith at all if the possibility of such subjective achievement of the feeling of knowledge were to be denied.

45. A faith that is spiritually demanded to be entertained cannot be taken to be incapable of being turned into knowledge. The moral postulates of Kant, for example, are such faiths. There is indeed no *moral* demand to entertain them, for they proceed from the demand for moral willing and there is no obligation on the part of the will to contemplate their objects. But when they have proceeded, are they mere speculative luxuries? Is the formulation of their objects with an *as though* spiritually indifferent or does it suggest a hope and a discipline to realize the hope of there being a grade of subjective realization higher than the moral? Such a grade may be admitted as "religion within the limits of pure reason" but the conceit of possible metaphysical knowledge, it may be said, need not, therefore, be reinstated. The conceit would be to Kant a moral impurity and critical honesty as essential to moral purity is essential to moral religion. But the conceit

that implies intellectual dishonesty is the belief that metaphysical reality is known, not that it is knowable. To take the spirit as finally known when its reality is to be achieved would be to take away the will to achieve. But if the spirit is believed to be unknowable, is not the will to achieve equally taken away? The will to realize the self, whether in knowledge or otherwise—for there may be different modes of realization—implies at any stage the knowledge of the self as not known and the belief that it is something more than as it is known. It cannot imply a belief in the self that is not knowledge at all, far less a belief in the self as unknowable.

46. The distinction of the object that is non-perceptually known from its knownness, presentation, or idea is just its character of being unknown which is believed and sought to be isolated by introspection. The known object is thus a problem to all knowledge other than perception. Perception is at once full knowledge, and restricted knowledge, full insofar as no lack of knowledge is felt in it and restricted because nothing beyond the object is necessarily suggested by it. In imaginative knowledge, as in higher forms of non-perceptual knowledge, there is a felt lack of intimacy with the object known while something is known in the object—its becoming before being, for example,—which is unknown in the sense of not being as evident as the perceived object and of being incapable of being perceived. It is believed as constituting the reality of the perceivable object, the object being its appearance which is not unreal and in this sense a phenomenon of the reality. Non-perceptual knowledge is thus knowledge of the object as phenomenal with belief in a reality constituting it.

47. There is no explicit belief in metaphysical reality except as thus implied in the knowledge of the phenomenal. To know the phenomenon is not *not* to know the reality but to know it as unknown and, it may be, as wanted to be known. Belief that is not knowledge at all is either unaccompanied by an idea of the object as distinct from the belief or is false belief. It is not possible, therefore, to say about the postulates of moral or aesthetic consciousness that they have only to be believed and cannot be known. They are, in fact, known as unknown, known as objects that are not to be rejected as permanent illusions but to be con-

templated as symbols of the reality to be known. What in the case of the understanding is known as phenomenon is in the case of the reason known as symbol, neither of which can be taken in our ordinary consciousness to be illusory though they would be realized as illusory if the reality that is known as unknown were to be completely known.

48. It would indeed be wrong to say that what is known as unknown is necessarily wanted to be known, that there is a necessity for the idea of a believed object to get transformed into knowledge. The knowledge of the unknown as such is the precondition as much of moral or aesthetic realization as of cognitive realization. It would be equally wrong on the other side to say that for non-cognitive realization it is necessary to give up faith in the knowability of the unknown. Belief in the unknowability of reality is not only not demanded; it is impossible and although in a sense the unknowable real can be conceived, the confusion of this mere conceiving with belief will exclude the possibility of all spiritual realization. We know or believe the reality to be unknown but we cannot believe it to be unknowable. We can doubt the knowledge of the phenomenon or symbol such as is implied in the knowledge of the unknown reality; but either such doubt does not amount to disbelief or if it does, the belief in the unknown reality also disappears, for that stands so long as the knowledge is not doubted. While the belief in the reality persists, the doubt is only an imaginary doubt, only the conceiving of a disbelief—no psychic fact at all but only a fringe of it—a conceiving of the totally unknown that is yet real. The concept of the totally unknown reality is the imaginary concept of the unknowable.

49. The factors of actual knowledge can never be proved to be necessary to all knowledge. A content that is claimed to be known may be shown afterwards to have been only believed or to be known as unknown but cannot be shown to be unknowable in the sense of being totally unknown and yet demanded to be believed. So long as it can be spoken of and believed, it is not to be regarded as totally unknown on the ground of some factor of actual knowledge being wanting. If the thing-in-itself or an Idea of Reason is spoken of and believed, it is already known as unknown; and because of the two factors of actual

object-knowledge—thought and intuition—either is wanting in this case, one has no right to doubt such knowledge as is there already or—what amounts to the same thing—to doubt the knowability of the unknown. To know something to be unknown implies, in fact, a demand to find a condition of its being known and if the conditions of other admitted knowledge be not there, it is a call to revise our epistemology and not to reject the knowledge of the unknown that sets the problem.

50. The knowledge of the unknown is what starts the actual problem of realization whether in the cognitive or in the non-cognitive direction. The demand for either mode of realization is absolute, though there is a spiritual choice—which is not merely the free choice of a will—between them. The non-cognitive mode does not entertain the demand that the unknown that is known as such should be known as known, that the belief in the reality has to be turned into the knowledge of it as evident. Not that it therefore demands that there should be a belief in its unknowability: it would, in fact, be impossible with such a belief. What is demanded for any mode of spiritual realization is that there should be the knowledge of a reality as beyond the known and that it should not be known as unknowable. The non-cognitive mode of realization does not demand the belief that it is the only mode and that the cognitive mode implies, as Kant would have it, a fanatical conceit or theosophic illusion. The impossibility of the cognitive mode would argue the impossibility of the non-cognitive modes as well.

51. Thus we meet the Kantian difficulty. Psychic fact, we said, involves presentation from which the perceivable object is distinct and which accordingly is object and more than object. It is *more* in the sense of being a metaphysical reality constitutive of the object which is its phenomenon, a reality that is known as unknown and as knowable, though the complete knowledge of it need not be demanded. Psychic fact as embodying belief in such reality is at once real and realizing, realizing as being already real, this being the objective counterpart of knowing the object as unknown. To Kant, metaphysical reality—what in presentation appears to be known as unknown in the object—is only thought and believed and appears to be known by an inevitable or perma-

nent illusion. We agree that the introspective awareness of the presentation as distinct from the object is not knowledge of knowing but only imagination of knowing the metaphysical. The imagination, however, is not an illusion but only incomplete or unrealized knowledge and hence the imagined knowing appears as the knowing of the unknown as such in the object. There is no question of turning this imagined knowing into actual knowing by sense-intuition: it can be actualized, if at all, by the concreting activity of imagination itself. Metaphysical reality is only symbolized in objective terms: it is not literally objective though the symbolizing may be a step toward knowledge of it as a subjective reality and need not be in the service of willing or feeling only. The subject may be sought to be realized morally or emotionally and the conceit of knowing the reality may be dropped but there is no necessity to drop it. Cognitive realization of the metaphysical reality as subjective has to be admitted, at least, as an alternative spiritual possibility.

52. In this cognitive realization, the knowledge of the unknown as such implies the demand to know the metaphysical reality not as an object hidden behind the perceivable object but as that of which the object is a free efflux and to know empirical fact as real not by being given but by the self-shining substantively existent cognition of it. What appear as characters of the object—characters like forming, pastness, or necessity revealed by imagination, memory, or inference—would in such realization cease to be adjectival and appear substantive. Psychic fact would not only appear isolated from its object in the stage of introspective realization proper to it but would cease to be distinguished from introspection as its object, shining out as a mode of introspection itself, as a self-evidencing functional fact. The phenomenal object—the object as imagined to be perceived—would appear to be a possibility that is not actual by its own right, being negated or turned into illusion in this sense though not in the sense that when put forth, it is not real at all.

53. Psychic fact appears to our ordinary unrealized introspection as more concrete than objective fact only in promise and not in actuality. It does not, however, appear as coordinate with

objective fact: it is what should be more real but is actually less real. To be more real is not to be a whole of which objective fact is an element, for the unobjective element of psychic fact that is known in introspection as the unknown character of the object is what constitutes the reality of the object. Psychic fact contains within it objective fact as a possibility but it would be wrong to say that the realization of the psychic *must* mean the actualization of this possibility. Actualization of a possible is, indeed, a necessity to knowing, provided we choose to know or to adopt the cognitive mode of realization. Object is a possibility within the psychic only in the sense that it *can* be actualized, not that it will or need be actualized. It is not comprehended in the psychic in the Hegelian sense.

54. The Indian conception of a specific activity of realization on the part of the individual spirit is alien to modern philosophy generally and specially to Hegelian philosophy. The individual spirit is supposed in the latter to be individual so far as he is subject and does not know his subjectivity objectively. He knows it objectively only as he finds it through non-cognitive spiritual activity. He asserts it non-cognitively but does not in such assertion will *toward* it as what is to be developed, does not know it and stand outside it in spiritual willing though in the consciousness of the resulting fulfillment, he knows the subjectivity to have been developed. To the absolute spirit, however, his will to realize his subjectivity is knowledge of his subjectivity *in* the willing and not *after* the willing: realization in the Indian sense is thus admitted in the absolute spirit alone. So far as it is admitted, it is understood as cognitive, non-cognitive activity being only a stage or constituent function in it. So the object, so far as it is known as unknown in the psychic state, would be taken by the Hegelian to be known by the individual as eternally known by the Absolute, as what not only can but will be unfolded by the psychic, being eternally unfolded in the Absolute. It is this necessity that is denied here as against the Hegelian: object as an ideality within the psychic is what can be unfolded but need not be. The psychic is more concrete than the object in the sense that it can freely put forth the lesser reality; and even as it does put forth, it does not

lend to it its whole reality but keeps itself still as more concrete than the manifested object. Nature is still to the Psyche a magic or playful appearance.

55. The parting from the Hegelian view is suggested at a comparatively late stage. But the view of the psychic as coordinate with the object and still more the view of it as comprehending the object as a real element have to be rejected at the very start. There is a tendency in certain recent developments of psychology to reject the ghostly psychic fact as coordinate with objective fact either in favor of an experience-unity of subject and object or in favor of the biological unity of the organism and its environment. We are not concerned with the latter for the present. The experience-unity of subject and object is supposed to be known in introspection. It is the psychic fact as implying the object as a real element, the presentation which is not not-object and from which the object is differentiated out by "intersubjective intercourse." Now the question is if this experience-unity is rightly claimed to be known by introspection, known so unambiguously that it can be proposed to be substituted for the current duality of subject and object. All that can be admitted is that we do not distinguish the presentation from the object as we distinguish the object from the presentation: we only cannot deny that the presentation is object though the object is other than presentation. The distinguishing of the object from its presentation is definite knowledge but the non-denial of the identity of presentation with its object does not amount to the knowledge of it. The presentation, in fact, cannot be known except as what the object is distinct *from*. By itself it is believed in introspection and it embodies belief in the object. Psychic fact as bound up with presentation cannot be asserted to *include* the object on the ground that presentation is not known as not-object or implies belief in the object.

56. The ordinary view of the ghostly psychic fact as coordinate with objective fact ignores the experienced non-distinction of presentation from its object while the view of experience-unity unwarrantably asserts it as identity. Is the duality of psychic fact and objective fact secured any better by the recognition of the distinction between the "enjoying" and the "contemplative"

modes of knowing? For one thing, it is doubtful if the enjoying knowledge of the psychic fact should be called knowledge at all. Even if it be taken as knowledge of it as objectively unknown, the difficulty is to relate the content of it with the content of contemplative knowledge. The distinction of objective fact from presentation or psychic fact may be taken to be itself an objective fact that is contemplatively known. But the distinction of psychic fact from the object, to be known, would have to be enjoyingly known. All that, however, can be said to be enjoyingly known is the psychic fact as distinct in itself. Its distinction from the object is only symbolically thought by an illegitimate extension of reversible character of the relation of distinction within contemplative knowledge. It is not known but is only a symbolism for the felt dissociation or freedom of the psychic fact from the object.

Chapter 3
Bodily Subjectivity

The Body as Perceived and Felt

57. Psychic fact has been taken to be fact of which we are introspectively aware as capable of existing apart from introspection. Introspection is the distinguishing of the presentation from its object, the object being given as distinct from the presentation. In perceptual knowledge, the object is not given as distinct from its presentation and hence perceptual knowledge is not at least directly the object of introspection and is not a psychic fact in this sense. We are, however, aware of the subject even in the subpsychic perceptual stage. The body as externally and internally perceived, as observed and felt, may be regarded as the subject in relation to the environment and psychology has to start with this bodily subjectivity.

58. The materialistic view that the subject is but the body is true insofar as the body represents a stage of being of the subject. But it ignores the unique singularity of one's own body even as a perceived object. No merely objectivistic account can do justice to this singularity. The objectivity of other perceived objects is constituted by their position relative to the percipient's body which itself, therefore, cannot be taken to be so constituted. To the percipient, his body is an object situated in space relatively to

some other percipient's body as imagined, being not perceived by himself in a space-position though not known, therefore, as non-spatial. The percipient as in his body or as his body is, in this sense, dissociated from the external world, being what his perceived world is distinct from. At the same time he cannot help imagining himself as included in the world though it may be as a privileged object.

59. One's own body is only half perceived, the rest being eked out by imagination. The unseen face of a solid object that is perceived is imagined by the percipient by imagining his own body being placed in a different position. To imagine the unseen half of one's own body, however, the observer does not imagine his own body thus placed differently. He imagines *another* observing body, not his own, as thus placed. In this respect also his own perceived body is uniquely different from other perceived objects and has no place in the objective world that he conceives to be presentable to him as a solipsistic observer. The world as a construction out of the views or perspectives of many observers cannot be simply identified with the world constructed out of the views of the same observer in different positions. The former is not, indeed, known as other than the latter; but it is a world organic to a subject that feels dissociated from his body, a world therefore that has no perceivable position and involves a space that he as percipient cannot take to be objective to him. Thus even if the subject is taken as nothing but one's own perceived body, it involves the knowledge of something unknown as such in the object, something that cannot be understood in terms of the perceptible object in the merely objectivistic attitude. It still implies the mystic awareness of dissociation from the object in which subjectivity consists. What is intended by the word *I* cannot be characterized even in the lowest stage of subjectivity as simply *this* object.

60. One's own body is not only perceived from outside: one is immediately or sensuously aware of it also from within in what is called "feeling of the body." This feeling is not, like the feeling of an object, a psychic fact from which the object known is distinguished. The bodily feeling is but the felt body which is not known to be other than the perceived body. Yet the perceived

body is distinct from it so far as it is an "interior" that is never perceived and cannot be imagined to be perceived from outside. Introspection, indeed, is sometimes taken as nothing but sense-perception of the interior of the body. But the interior cannot be understood here as the interior that one may imagine oneself seeing. To say that it is the same spatial interior, only appearing indefinite, is to ignore the qualitative difference that is felt between the indefiniteness of a perceived position and the indefiniteness of a felt position, the position, for example, of a pain in the perceived body. Our knowledge of objective space may have been developed from the felt spread of the body or the felt location in it but we are always aware of such felt space as only *partially* defined into perceived space and, therefore, cannot assert the former to be nothing more than the latter. Perceived space, however it may be extended and complicated by the geometric imagination, can at best symbolize the uniquely felt space that sets the problem of objective interpretation and is always in advance of the interpretation. It is even as the uniquely singular *I* is symbolized by the objectively singular *this*, being never adequately interpreted by it.

61. Objective space that is indefinitely perceived is the same as the objective space that is definitely perceived and the definition does not involve any fresh objectification. But felt space is indefinite in the sense that it is more than the objective space it is defined into, *more* in the sense already explained in which the presentation of an object is more than the object. The felt interior of the body may thus be regarded as the prototype of the observable interior, not merely the latter as presented indefinitely but what can only be symbolized by the latter in its full definiteness. Definite objective space is related to felt space as the objective exterior is related to the objective interior, the latter relation being, in fact, the reflection of the former relation.

62. The awareness of the body from within is, indeed, sensuous but it can hardly be called sense-perception. It is only not denied to be perception, though the perceived body as an object among objects is distinguished from the body as felt from within. The body is felt as extending from a vague interior to the outer

surface that may be both felt and perceived. But the perception of the body stops at the surface and if it is extended by the imagination of the interior, the interior is still imagined as an external surface. The perceived and imagined body is always an exterior which may also be felt but the felt interior can never be imagined as perceived. Thus the felt body cannot be distinguished from the perceived body though the latter is distinguished from the former.

63. The relation between the felt body and the perceived body is similar to the relation of presentation and its object in non-perceptual knowledge. There is, however, the difference that introspection into such knowledge is possible because the presentation is felt to be dissociated though not known to be distinct from its object while there is no introspection into body-feeling, as we are not aware of it as dissociated from the perceived body. Body-feeling and felt body are only verbally distinct; and the awareness of the felt body is not the awareness of anything but the perceived body though the perceived body is distinguished from the felt body. As in the case of the perception of objects, there is no conscious duality of presentation and object in body-feeling and as in the case of non-perceptual knowledge, the perceptible object—here the body—is distinguished from something which however here is the felt body and not presentation and is not suspected like presentation as the possibility of anything other than the perceived body. Body-feeling may accordingly be regarded as not psychic fact but the potentiality of it. The problem of dissociating it from the objective body does not yet arise, as it arises in the case of psychic fact. But the possibility of dissociation is there, in the actualization of which body-feeling may be conceived to be transformed into psychic fact. Actually in body-feeling, we are not interested in withdrawing from the environment: it is only an interest derived from higher stages of subjectivity that suggests such withdrawal.

64. We may consider body-feeling in relation to psychic fact and introspection into psychic fact on the one hand and to the perceived body and perceived object on the other. The perceived body is only potentially dissociated from the perceived object inasmuch as it is not merely like presentation not denied to be

object but is positively known as object. There is no explicit awareness of dissociation from the object but since position relative to the body, which is a constitutive character of the object, may not be analyzed out in perception, the object is only half distinguished from the body, the body being, therefore, only implicitly or potentially dissociated from it. The object, however, is fully distinguished from the felt body: the perceived object presents exterior surface only, its so-called interior being, as perceived or imagined to be perceived, still an exterior. Corresponding to this full distinction from the felt interior, there is the actual but imperfect dissociation or freedom of the felt body from the perceived environment. The felt body, however, does not appear even imperfectly dissociated from the perceived body. It is only potentially dissociated because the perceived body is half distinguished from the felt body in the sense one who observes his body as exterior to him may not feel it.

65. Again, the perceived body is fully distinguished from psychic fact—from the imagination of the body, for example—which however is imperfectly but consciously dissociated from it. There may be consciousness of the body as *mine* and at the same time as not other than myself, unlike the consciousness of the object which if felt as *mine* is felt as not *me*. The felt body is, however, only half distinguished from psychic fact, since it is the feeling of the body on the one hand and is not actually dissociated from the perceived body on the other. Psychic fact accordingly is only potentially or implicitly and not actually or explicitly dissociated from the felt body. In introspection into psychic fact, this potential dissociation of the psychic fact from the felt body becomes imperfectly actual: there is no awareness of the psychic fact as not involving bodily feeling at all though bodily feeling as the felt body itself is other than the psychic fact. The felt body begins to get resolved into a bodiless psychic feeling in introspection and may be conceived to be fully resolved when introspection gets realized as assured knowledge. Meantime our ordinary introspection involves awareness of the felt body as not other than the perceived body from which, however, psychic fact is felt to be completely detached. It is in this sense only that introspection may be taken as the sense-

perception of the bodily interior. Strictly speaking, it is the awareness of a psychic fact felt as fully detached from the perceived body or the bodily exterior and half detached from the felt bodily interior which also is half detached from the bodily exterior.

66. The facthood of the subjective is constituted by this feeling of detachment or freedom. The first hint of this freedom is reached in the feeling of the body. In the perception of the object, there need not be the knowledge of the object being distinct from the body. Developed perception may involve such knowledge but still the body is taken as perceived object. When the perceived body is distinguished from the felt body, the exterior from the interior, we have an explicit feeling of distinction, detachment, or freedom from the perceived object. Apart from the specific activity of realization which subjectivity suggests, the first given feeling of freedom in body-feeling is what all freedom of higher grade involves and derives its meaning from. Subjectivity apart from spiritual discipline is rooted in body-feeling and is only imagined to be dissociable from it. Psychic fact is then fact because of the knowledge of object or the presentation that it involves, because of the consequent felt detachment of it from the perceived body and of its non-detachment from the felt body. In introspection, indeed, there is the initial detachment of psychic fact from the felt body but introspection itself is fact only as a fringe of some psychic fact which is undetached from the felt body. This initial detachment here is only imagined, for the felt body is not yet turned into a psychic feeling, introspection being only the faith that the detachment can be realized. The realization of this freedom from the felt body is the pre-condition of all distinctively spiritual activity.

Chapter 4
Bodily Subjectivity (Cont.)

Knowledge of Absence as a Present Fact

67. The perception of objective fact does not imply a distinguishing of the object from the presentation of it. That there is a presentation here from which the object is distinct is not directly known by introspection. Perception as a psychic fact is known only in introspection into non-perceptual knowledge. In memory, for example, there is the distinguishing of the past object from the presentation (image) of it and in introspection into memory, there is the further distinguishing of the past perceptual presentation of the object from the present image of it, the object being thus known as having been unconsciously distinct from the past presentation. The perceived object may, however, be directly distinguished from the felt body which, as has been pointed out, is like the perceived object undistinguished from presentation but yet involves a feeling of detachment from all object other than perceived body. The feeling of the body may accordingly be taken to be an implicate of developed perception, of the perception of the object as distinct from the felt body, and to be only a fringe of perceptual knowledge. The knowledge of absence as a present fact that now comes up for discussion is similarly a fringe of object-perception of a higher grade, involv-

ing like all perception no distinction of the fact from the presentation of it. The absence of object that is immediately known as a
present fact is just midway between the body felt to be present
and the presentation that is felt to be detached from present fact
in non-perceptual knowledge.

68. Objective fact may be said to be present as external, as
internal, and as absent. The felt body is objective fact in its
internal aspect. An object may be also directly known to be *now*
absent, to be "present as absent" in this sense—a paradoxical
phrase to be justified presently. All these three aspects may be
said to be known in connection with sense and involve no distinguishing from presentation. A present object as external may be
distinguished from other present objects as external, from a present object as internal, or from the present absence of itself. The
feeling of the body is already a detachment from the external
object though not from the body as external. The direct knowledge of the present absence of an object is a detachment not only
from the object but also from the perceived body though not from
the body as internally felt. The absence of an object, so far as it is
located, is located like its presence in reference to the body but the
reference is in opposite directions. The object as present is there
away from my body. In the case of absence, the object being
missed or unreached by my body is what my body is away from:
the absence is where my body is not. Thus the body as external is
distinguished from the object as absent and not the latter from the
former. Corresponding to this distinction, there is the felt detachment from the body of the present absence of the object or of
the object as now missed, the consciousness of the absence or the
absent being thus removed from the space round the body.

69. The sense-conditioned knowledge of an object being now
absent is not to be confused with the memory, expectation, or
imagination of the object. None of these need involve knowledge
of its *present* absence. An object may be remembered, expected,
or imagined though it is now present: non-perceptual knowledge
of it may coexist with perceptual knowledge. There are cases,
again, in which there is no distinct image of the absent object at all
and where yet we may be aware of the perceived locus of the
absence as empty or devoid of an indefinite something. A con-

sciously imagined object as now absent or the absence of an object not consciously imagined that characterizes a perceived locus as empty is known in connection with sense and known, if not in perception, in a cognitive mode undissociated from perception. The cognition is a fringe either of the perception of the locus or of the perception of the body and is in either case undissociated from the feeling of the body.

70. The cognition of an object as now absent may but need not involve the cognition of its absence as characterizing a locus and the latter also may but need not involve the former. The two cognitions are, therefore, distinct and each as primary may involve the latter as secondary. A field, for example, was observed in the past with a tree standing on it, which might not have been particularly noticed at the time. The observer comes to the place when the tree has been removed and finds a new bare look about the place. He may not know that it is absence of the tree that makes the difference but he notices the difference, bareness or absence. To take another example, a person is looking for a book in a room but does not find it. He knows the book to be absent without being conscious of any empty look about the room and without, in fact, consciously referring the absence to the room at all. The former example would be a case of cognition of the *absence* of an object (tree) and the latter of cognition of an object (book) being *absent*. Neither cognition here need imply the other and both are direct sense-conditioned cognitions of objective fact. Yet each may develop into the other cognition: what is absent may come to be realized as tree in the first example and the absence of the book may come to be realized in explicit reference to the room in the second.

71. Should the primary and secondary cognitions in each case be called perception? In the first case, the absence of the tree is known as a character of the locus, the perceived field where the tree stood. The tree may not be definitely remembered but if remembered it is recognized to be the specification of the absence that continues to be known, the place not ceasing to wear the bare look because of the definite memory. As the place is perceived, absence as a character of the place may also be claimed to be perceived. There is, however, a distinction between the sense in

which absence is a character and that in which a quality like color is a character of the place. The place in being perceived with the bareness or absence is, if not perceived, at least imagined as what need not have the character, being presented as with a new look or, in other words, as distinct from what it might be. But to perceive the place with a color is not necessarily to imagine that it might be without it. The perceived locus of absence being imagined in the very perception of it as without the absence, the absence is only a floating adjective that unlike color is felt to be dissociated from the locus. There is a suggestion of the absence being outside the space where the locus stands—the space round the body, of its being *nowhere* like an image, though it is believed to be objective and not psychic fact. The suggestion is not actual imagination of positionless objective fact but only the attempted symbolizing of the feeling of detachment from objective space. The absence cannot be said to be not known as objective but it is implicitly felt to be dissociated from objective space. The perception of it as a character of the object in the feeling that it is not a character and with the conscious distinguishing of the object from it may be called aesthetic or imaginative perception to distinguish it from ordinary perception.

72. In the second example, what is known in the first instance is not the absence of the book but the book as absent. The book is not found and the room where it is not found is not perceived, at least immediately, to have any empty look owing to the absence. The book as absent is immediately known as a present objective circumstance that is neither remembered nor merely imagined. The missing of the imagined book is a characteristic experience, implying a feeling of the body not reaching it, which is interpreted as the objective fact of the book being absent. The knowledge of this fact of the book as absent is with the conscious imagination of the book as found being distinct from it and implies the feeling of the present fact being outside objective space altogether. Such knowledge also may, therefore, be called aesthetic or imaginative perception. The difference from the previous case is that what is imaginatively distinguished within the perception is not the perceived locus of the absence from the absence but the imagined object-as-present from the perceived

object-as-absent. In neither case is the positive object distinguished from a presentation as in non-perceptual knowledge. It is distinguished in both cases from the objective fact of absence or the absent and not from a psychic fact. This objective fact that is distinguished from may thus be said to be perceived.

73. The primary cognitions of absence and the absent which are both perception may be followed by secondary cognitions. The perception of the absence of the tree in the first example may develop into the cognition of the tree as absent and the perception of the book as absent in the second example into the cognition of the absence of the book imagined explicitly as the book *in the room*. The interest may shift in the former case from the bare look of the locus to what was in it but is no longer existing and in the latter case from the book that is missed to the locus which might have been but is not with the object. Are these secondary cognitions also perception?

74. When after the perception of the absence of the tree as a character of the place, the tree as remembered is known to be now absent, there is no missing of a looked-for object like the missing of the book in the second example. If an object is looked for and not found, the object as it might be now, with presentness as its adjective, is perceived to be absent. Again, when absence is known as a character or adjective of a present locus, it is taken to be perceived. But when as in this case *that* object tree is known to be *now* absent, the presentness is not adjective either to the object or to the locus but is only an adverbial mode of the adjective *absent*. What is consciously referred to as *now* is neither the object nor the locus but the absence only. *That* object is not now perceivable and the perception of this place is irrelevant to the knowledge of the tree as absent. Such knowledge is not perception: there is no perception that is not or does not consciously imply apprehension of a concrete as present.

75. The secondary cognition of *that* tree as now absent is not perception, though it is immediate and sense-conditioned cognition of the present. What is known to be *now* absent is known in the consciousness of not perceiving it, with the belief that it would have been perceived had it been present. Not that it is,

therefore, *inferred* to be absent: the consciousness of not perceiving what, it is inferred, would have been perceived is itself no inference and is at once the objective knowledge of the present fact of absence. Present absence by itself is then immediately known in connection with sense and inference by what may be called conscious non-perception. This has to be recognized as a new mode of knowledge and is comparable with the pure perception of object, conceived as that to which the object is not given but before which it floats up like an image and is nonetheless believed. Conscious non-perception is, indeed, in connection with sense but what is perceived by sense is irrelevant to its content.

76. The secondary cognition in the second example is also a case of conscious non-perception. To make it more readily intelligible, we may vary the illustration and consider the absence of a beloved person instead of a book that is looked for in a room. When such a person is missed or imaginatively perceived as now absent, there may not be any relevant reference to the locus, namely, the room. But one may come to imagine the room as with the person and then realize his absence in reference to this imagined content. To imagine an object in a perceived locus is a special form of imagination in which the present locus is viewed as characterizing and not as characterized by the imagined content. The belief in the absence of the object as thus characterized by the locus, the absence here of the imagined room as sentimentally associated with the beloved person, is immediate knowledge but not perception. The absence is not taken to be fact *in* the present locus; and as the presentness of the absence is not the presentness of any concrete thing, it cannot be said to be perceived. The secondary cognition is conscious non-perception, the room that is perceived by sense being turned into the imagined character of location of the imagined person.

77. The primary cognition of absence and the absent is imaginative perception and the secondary cognition of them is conscious non-perception. The relation of these modes of cognition with the apprehension of the body has now to be brought out. The primary cognition is related to the perception of the body as the

secondary cognition is related to the feeling of the body. The absence of the tree in the first example is where its locus is. The tree as absent, however, is not essentially referred to the locus, being felt in fact as outside the space round my body, as detached from reference to the perceived body. The positionlessness is felt and believed as a mode of my body-feeling which is dissociated from the object. The *now* or presentness of the absence is the *now* or the presentness of the body-feeling. But while the *now* of the body-feeling is not distinguished from the *then* as remembered or the *might be* as imagined, being only an implicit *now*, the *now* of the absent tree in this case is so distinguished. The *absent-now* is felt dissociated from the perceived body as the felt body is not. Thus the felt body is imperfectly distinct from the *absent-now* which, therefore, only appears to be a mode of the felt body, being undetached from it but really represents a stage higher and just falling short of the detached image. There is a similar relation of the primary and secondary cognitions in the second example to the perceived body and the felt body.

78. In the imaginative perception of absence and the absent, there is no explicitly felt dissociation from the position of the perceived body, which however is imperfectly distinguished from the imagined position of absence or of the absent. In conscious non-perception, there is the explicitly felt dissociation from the perceived body but not from the felt body, though the felt body has begun to be distinguished from the fact of absence or the absent. The relation of the perceived body in the former case and of the felt body in the latter to the known absence is like the relation of the perceived body to the felt body. The perceived body is half distinguished from the felt body which, however, is not felt to be dissociated from the perceived body. Absence imaginatively perceived is thus on a level with the felt body, both being felt undissociated from the perceived body which however is half distinguished from them. Absence known by conscious non-perception is on a higher level, being felt half dissociated from the perceived body which, however, is fully distinguished from it and undissociated from the felt body which is half distinguished from it.

79. Conscious non-perception then is a transitional stage between body-feeling and imagination with which psychic fact begins. It is the consciousness of presentness without space-position, the same as the presentness of the felt body but distinguished from such absence of the perceived object as is realized in imagination, memory, or expectation as the *might be*, the past, or the future. It is free from space but not from the present and accordingly does not imply a presentation of the object as dissociated from the object. Psychic fact begins with the distinguishing of what the present is not. Conscious non-perception is the distinguishing of the present from the detached presentation and not reversely and may be taken as the immediate pre-condition of the felt detachment of the presentation from the present. Were one to start with object-perception as the actual standard of knowledge, the first clear hint of the subjective fact would be realized in the knowledge of absence through conscious non-perception.

Chapter 5
Psychic Subjectivity

The Image

80. Psychology does not begin till the perceived object is distinguished from the half perceived body. The body may not be felt as dissociated from the objective world but it is still realized as a uniquely central object round which the world is disposed. To those who would not go further in psychology, introspection is only observation of the indefinite body-interior and psychic fact is only a bodily attitude, the beginning of the behavior of an organism to the environment. Some, however, would go one step further and admit the image as a unique fact, appearing as a quasi-object from which object including the body is distinguished. Psychology to them cannot ignore the image, even if it be only ancillary to bodily behavior. The image may be functional in character as a reference to the object, the reference being ultimately a behaving mode; but that it appears presented as a substantive something from which the object is distinct and exists in a sense in which the object does not exist cannot be denied.

81. The meaning of facthood appears to change as we pass from the perceived object as fact to the image as fact. This is realized if we interpose between them the three entities so far discussed—the perceived body, the felt body, and absence of

object as known in conscious non-perception. Each later term in the series appears to be fact in a sense different from the term before it—the perceived body from the perceived object, the felt body from the perceived body and so on. Facthood as an abstraction has an unformed symbolic meaning: its actual meaning depends on the nature of the content that is taken as fact. Fact in general means only what is believed or asserted but what fact means as a predicate applied to a content apart from the subjective function of assertion is indeterminate. Its meaning depends on the form of knownness of the content, the knownness that is its constitutive character and is abstracted by the so-called psychological introspection. The object is object to us so far as it is given and not self-evident like I, so far as it is presented and believed as more than it is known, so far, in fact, as it is known to be unknown. Knownness as an abstraction emerges only with this positive awareness of the unknown and has meaning only in reference to it. If the abstraction by itself has a meaning, it stands for an indeterminate which is not given nor yet is self-evidencing like the knowing I, being at best what is to be known. The concept of fact in general or knownness by itself is thus a problem in meaning and not an accomplished meaning. Meantime facthood is but a name for many grades or modes of fact which have no *actual* relation of similarity or point of similarity. We have accordingly to begin by accepting the different grades of fact as implying different meanings of facthood.

82. A perceived object is necessarily a spatial object having a position relatively not only to other perceived objects but also to the percipient's body. The perceived parts of his body are to him like outside objects situated relatively to some part of his body that he does not perceive nor even imagine himself perceiving but imagines only as perceivable (by another) and yet as continuous with the part that he perceives. His perceivable body as a whole is not perceived by him as situated relatively to the object. The perceived positional relation of one object to another is reversible but that of the object to the percipient's body as a whole is not reversible. Position relatively to the percipient's body is a character that constitutes the facthood of the perceived object, but his body as a perceivable fact is not constituted to his percep-

tion by position relative to the object though it is imagined by him as situated relatively to another spectator in a perceived objective position. This lack of perceived position is what distinguishes the facthood of one's perceivable body from the facthood of the objects perceived by him.

83. The imagined position of the perceived body is in objective space, space that is all exterior to the actual or imaginary percipient. Interior and exterior within objective space are understood relatively to two spectators: what the same actual spectator perceives is only the exterior. What he apprehends as interior is the felt space: his felt position consists in withdrawal from objective space, though it is not known as other than the imagined position of the perceivable body. The body is still felt to have a position which objective position is not but which is not, therefore, known as other than objective position. The interiority of the felt body is what distinguishes its existence from that of the perceived body.

84. The absence of an object is immediately known as a present objective fact. Has its facthood any reference to space-position? In what we have called the aesthetic or imaginative perception of absence, the absence is taken to be where the thing absent is imagined to be. Now in imagining an object in a perceived position, the position is turned into an imagined character of the object. The position of the absence of the object is thus imagined though not imaginary. The position of the perceived body is also imagined and of both it may be said that they are not unperceived because imagined, being, in fact, perceived through the imagination. The difference is that the body is half perceived by sense while the absence is perceived wholly through imagination. Absence has a factual position only as the felt body is undetached from the perceiving body. The position of absence as distinguished from the absence itself, is like the perceivable body half perceived through the imagination: the locus is perceived by sense and it is also imagined as turned into a character of the imagined object. Perceived absence then is on a level with the felt body but its position is on the level of the perceived body. Such absence is undetached from its position as the felt body is undetached from the perceived body.

85. Absence that is known by conscious non-perception is not referred to objective space. It is not known as with a position though it would be going too far to say that it is known as positionless. It is felt even as the body is felt, the belief in it being a bodily feeling of not feeling the object. Yet as the felt body is not detached from the perceived body and appears spatial as the mystic interior, absence in conscious non-perception is referred to this interior. It is as though the absent object was in the felt body. Yet the felt body is half distinguished from it, just as the perceived body is half distinguished from the felt body. Absence is here not known as with position while the felt body is known as with an unknown position from which objective space-position is distinct. There is the further distinction that the presentness of the absence is asserted explicitly while bodily feeling is only the implicit feeling of presentness. It is the explicit presentness that makes it possible for absence to be known as objective and yet without position.

86. The image is known to be without position while absence in conscious non-perception is only not known with position. So, too, absence is known as present or *now,* while the image is not known as *now.* The image has no space-position and it cannot be asserted to have a time-position, which, however, is not denied. To imagine an object is not necessarily to know it as now absent. We may imagine it while we perceive it, for example, when the object is our body and we may perceive it wholly through imagination as in what has been called aesthetic perception. But we imagine the object also when we know it to be absent. In such a case we imperfectly distinguish the object as *now* absent from the image of the object, which however is undissociated from the absent object and as such is not denied to be *now* but is not, therefore, asserted to be *now.*

87. The ordinary perception of object is said to involve imagination but the image here is only inferred and cannot appear to introspection. In a perception like that of one's own body, there is the direct consciousness of something in it as not sensed, from which the sensed portion of the body is distinguished but which itself is not distinguished from it. In what has been called aesthe-

tic or imaginative perception, not only is the sense-perceived locus of its object distinguished from it: the object as imaginatively perceived is distinguished from itself as merely imagined though not conversely. In none of these cases is the image felt to be dissociated from the percept. In the knowledge of absence through conscious non-perception, the image of the absent object is felt to be dissociated from the felt body but not from the present absence. What is known to be wholly distinct from the image at this stage is the object as present and not as absent. The knowledge of present absence is still a mode of bodily subjectivity; but in imagination as a free psychic fact, even the present absence is distinguished from the image; and so the image, though not explicitly dissociated from the presentness, is not known as with this character which is the last vestige of perceptible facthood. The image here appears with objective form but does not appear with objective position.

88. The relation of the image and of psychic fact generally to objective time has been the subject of controversy. There is the current banality that psychic facts are only in time while objective facts are in both space and time. We have pointed out on the one hand that absence that is known in conscious non-perception is not known to be in space though it is objective and that the image proper on the other is not known to be in time. We cannot assert nor can we deny that such objective absence is in space and that the image is in time. The image is assertable as not in space, neither in perceptible space nor in felt space. It has, indeed, spatiality as a character or form; and it is even possible to imagine an object on a perceived locus, where, however, the image is not in space but has space-position as an aesthetic expression. Thus there is a felt dissociation of the image from objective space and even from the felt interior of the body. Since the absence known in conscious non-perception is not consciously dissociated from the felt body, it is only half distinguished from the image, being not deniable as in space while the image is so deniable; and thus the image is not felt dissociated from the present absence though it is potentially dissociated.

89. This potential dissociation of the image from the *now* is

realized in "thought." In the examples of non-perception so far given it has been assumed that the object that is absent is imaged. But there may be cases where the absent object is only thought, as for example, when we say "no man is present here": man in general is here thought and not imaged. The vague image of an individual man may float up but the absence that is known is the absence not of this man in particular but of all men. The image here as symbolizing the thought may be said to be consciously dissociated from the presentness of the absence. Thus though the image need not be denied as *now*, it may be denied. We cannot assert that the image of the object now absent is *now* and we can in higher stages, for example, in the stage of image with thought definitely deny it.

90. The lowest stage of psychic fact is represented by the image without thought, emerging in the conscious non-perception of the absent as such. Just as the perception of the object half-consciously implies the perception of the body, this the feeling of the body and this again the conscious non-perception of the absent, so this last implies the image of the absent from which the absent as such is imperfectly distinguished. Attention here is primarily directed to the objective absence but in distinguishing it we attend indirectly to the image of the object that is absent. As thus indirectly attended to, the image is not distinguished and appears without thought. There is no awareness yet of its being not objective: it appears as a ghostly object that does not consciously imply belief, much as the half perceived body appears when an object is perceived to be *there*. The awareness of the image is still bound up with the perceiving attitude and is not introspective. The image is still consciously as though it were an object. It is like the illusion of the object persisting after correction, though it is only without belief and does not imply as in the case of illusion a conscious disbelief. It is only potentially psychical, being an object for possible introspection.

91. The distinguishing of the presentation of an object from the object is introspection which does not amount to the knowledge of the presentation as a given distinct. The distinguishing of the object from its presentation is, however, a phase of object-

knowledge. The presentation as thus distinguished from is an indefinite quasi-object. It is felt dissociated from the object as having no position in objective space and except in its lowest phase as image is felt also as not in time. In the case of the image, there is only no consciousness of its being an event in time: it is not felt to be not in time. Conscious non-perception of an object implies, indeed, the conscious image of the object but what is believed to be present fact is the *object* as absent, as distinct from the image which is neither believed nor disbelieved to exist at the moment. In the thought of an objective fact, however, the meaning which is the presentation is not only not referred to time: its existence in time is meaningless.

92. In conscious non-perception of an object, its image is not directly attended to and there is no introspective distinguishing of it from the object as absent. When it is introspectively attended to, it changes its character; the image appears as imaging, as being formed though not as unformed, as functional without ceasing to be substantive. A presentation like meaning also appears functional under introspection but loses its substantive character. The completed meaning is turned into the meaning act and loses its ghostly objectivity. All psychic fact conceived in introspection to be outside introspection is the quasi-objective fact of presentation which, however—with the exception of the image—appears as a mere function or act under introspection. The ghostly psychic fact cannot accordingly be taken to be a mere illusion; it is what introspection testifies to as existing consciously outside itself and the lowest form of it, namely, the image is apprehended even in the objective attitude apart from the testimony of introspection. The view of psychic life as the self's transaction with quasi-objective presentation is suggested by the image. A presentation like meaning that wholly melts into function under introspection does not stand before the self as object for its attention.

93. The image appears under introspection as functional and substantive at the same time, as a form being formed. This forming or incomplete character of the image requires fuller consideration than it has received. There is a qualitative difference between

the incompleteness of an image and the incompleteness of a perceived object, much like the difference between felt space and perceived space. The incompleteness of a percept is in reference to a fuller percept; taken by itself, a percept is finished and definite and an indefinite and unfinished sense-appearance is not yet a percept. The sense-given cannot be incomplete in itself without being indefinite and without falling short of a percept. The image, however, is incomplete not merely in comparison with a percept but in itself; it could not, in fact, be complete without being a percept. There cannot be a finished form that is not believed as the form of a perceived object. The imagined form is always being formed without, however, being indefinite like the sense-given content which is being formed into a percept. It is definite because the consciousness of the forming is at once the consciousness of the form to be completed. The forming and the form appear to be seen together, as they are actually seen together in what has been called aesthetic or imaginative perception. The image under introspection is, in fact, a standing process where the forming is not chronologically prior to the form and yet appears distinct from the form which is its interpretation. Under introspection accordingly the image appears as not in time while the image before introspection, as in the stage of conscious non-perception, is only not known to be in time. The consciousness of the finished form that interprets the forming is sometimes called *idea*. But the idea at this stage is not a separate presentation but only a fringe of the image. It is not dissociated from the image as forming, which, however, is distinguished from it. The idea as dissociated from the image would be the next psychic stage.

Chapter 6
Psychic Subjectivity (Cont.)

Thought

94. The image under introspection appears as a forming form in which the finished form is evident in the forming process as its interpreting idea. The idea as dissociated from the image is idea of the object as not imaged and sought to be imaged. The object here appears indefinite and the imagining or forming that is started by the conscious want of the image is the process of defining it. This process which may be called the materializing of the dissociated idea is intrinsically incomplete and is ever to be completed. The undissociated idea of the previous stage is the complete form that as much appears to be seen as the incomplete forming. The dissociated idea thus implies the imaging process and the conscious want of the image. The want is here only partial but there may be idea of something in the object that cannot be defined or concreted into image at all. Such idea is thought proper that is definite in itself and is not defined in meaning but at best fixed or detained in the mind by the images it may still call up. The images here have a consciously metaphorical or symbolizing value for the idea.

95. Image or thought here is considered as presentation that embodies or at least does not exclude belief in the object. The

mere image or the mere meaning, the object of which is disbelieved from the start is, as indicated before, no psychic fact at all. Now what in the object is believed specifically through imagination—namely, the form—though not posited in the space that is organic to the body, is still represented as spatial, appearing as though it were felt like the body. What is believed specifically through thought, however, does not thus appear to be intimately felt and is yet as definite as the imagined form. The dissociated idea lies midway between the definite form and the definite intelligible, being non-spatial in form but indefinite and only partially definable by an incomplete forming. It may be called pictorial thought to distinguish it from thought proper, the object of which is definitely presented as unpicturable meaning. Picturable metaphors and symbols may be used to fix the identity of such meaning and for purposes of easy communication but they do not help to define or elaborate it.

96. The image lacks space-position but still appears spatial in form and temporal as forming or becoming and as such implies a belief in its possible objectivity. Thought as the awareness of the unimaginability of its specific content is the awareness of its objectivity being impossible and thus involves a complete detachment from objectivity. Thought is still about the object but it is of something about the object that is definitely unobjective. In lower stages and even in the stage of body-feeling, something unobjective in the object is also presented but it is not known explicitly to be unobjective, not completely denied as objective. It is completely denied in thought and if it is still said to be something in the object, it is understood to be what *appeared* as objective, what the object was not distinguished from in the lower stages. The thinkable universal or relation, for example, was presented as objective in the lower stages and the object was never sufficiently distinguished from that presentation. Even in the stage of pictorial thought or the dissociated idea, the universal appeared as a quasi-spatial whole and relation as a quasi-temporal transition. In non-pictorial thought, this conceit of their quasi-objectivity is dropped, though the object continues to be referred to as what exists and is known without name and with-

out relation. The universal and relation in the object are recognized, if not as thinking, as not distinguished from thinking, the object given as distinct being reduced to unrelated singulars or unique contents such as may be conceived to be "purely perceived." As thus referring to the object, meaning is still objective though explicitly through thinking, being a presentation and not a free subjectivity.

97. Non-pictorial thought which is definite independently of the image may be sought to be metaphorically or symbolically indicated by the image. Metaphor differs from symbol: the object that is thought is imagined as though it were the same as the metaphor but not as though it were the same as the symbol. Both are recognized to be to other than the object thought; but while the metaphor is consciously employed as similar to the object, the symbol which is also remotely similar to the object in relational constitution is not employed *as* similar. The word is a symbol and not a metaphor for the object meant; the metaphor is only half distinguished from the meaning while the symbol is fully distinguished. Thought in its higher grade is detained in the mind by the word and not by its figurative representation.

98. Thought as distinct from the forming image under introspection is a completed product and the thinking that does not amount to a complete thought is a misnomer and should only be called a trying to think. This complete thought is about an object and the object thought is quite definite, whatever indefiniteness or incompleteness there may be in the symbolic imaging of it. Thought is complete as dissociated altogether from time, not merely from time-position from which the image (at least under introspection) is also dissociated but also from the forming or ideal timing that characterizes the image. It is complete in the sense of being eternal; and spatial or temporal objectivity is distinguished from it. Still thought is about the object and as such should be called "presentation." Its content is such as is *necessarily* characterized as what the object is distinct from. Thought is thus a psychic fact, having a facthood apart from introspection. Despite its eternity, it would be incorrect to speak of it as a pure subjective activity. Much of the mysticism in

Kantio-Hegelian philosophy has sprung from the confusion of thought with pure subjective activity, of reason with the spirit. Compared with the awareness of *I*, thought is objective and objective in its very dissociation from objectivity. It has still to be characterized in reference to the object as what the object is not.

99. That thought is a presentation comes out in the form of consciousness which we have called *trying* to think. Thought outside introspection is the accomplished meaning. The meaning stands in higher thought, at any rate, through the word. The word is quite distinct from the meaning but as *being used*, it is only half distinguished from the meaning while the meaning is not dissociated at all from it within thought. The identity of the meaning with the word cannot be denied though it would be going too far to assert it. The identity is disturbed in the consciousness of missing the meaning of a word-combination of which the constituents have a meaning. The problem as to what a combination of significant words means, if it means anything, is an intelligible problem and so attained meaning is distinguished from possible meaning. Attained meaning has accordingly a kind of being outside subjective activity and is a presentation in this sense.

100. What, however, is this possible meaning, the missing of an actual meaning, the trying to think? The logical form of word-combination or syntactical connection is a generality that has no actual meaning apart from the constituent words but cannot be denied to have a meaning when the word-combination has a meaning from which the meanings of the constituent words can be distinguished. The form of connection here is not itself distinguished as an actual meaning, being only distinguished from. As itself distinguished, it is possible meaning; and in the problem of finding the meaning of a word-combination, the possible meaning is what symbolizes the lack of actual meaning. Within thought, the image or the word furnishes the symbolism but here the form of thought itself constitutes the symbol for the felt problem. The feeling of the problem with the unrejected active faith in its solubility is the trying to think which is beyond thought or meaning, beyond all presentation.

Chapter 7
Spiritual Subjectivity

Feeling

101. Thought is still presented as meaning, as the unobjective something about the object, being characterizable only in reference to the object as what the object is not. The introspective awareness of meaning as distinct from the image is awareness of the explicitly unobjective. Feeling is also explicitly unobjective but it is not merely negative but positive as *subjective* fact without any reference to objective fact. The thought of object may accompany a feeling but it is recognized as only a symbolism for the feeling, as what no longer intends the object, being not consciousness of *object* as unknown but an avowedly over-definite representation of the merely unknown. The consciousness of the merely unknown as distinct from what is known as object that is also unknown is feeling. The consciousness may be called knowledge, such knowledge as has been sometimes supposed to constitute dreamless sleep. It is purely subjective in the sense that there is no conscious reference to object even in the way of dissociation from it though not yet in the sense that the meanability or thinkability of its specific content is denied. Feeling is as much undissociated from its content "absence of knowledge" as conscious non-perception is undissociated from the objective

absence that is its content. In the *trying* to think, as in feeling, thought is distinguished from the conscious absence of thought which itself is not distinguished from thought. While however in the trying, there is no belief in the unmeant as a distinct content, feeling involves such belief, much as perception involves belief in an object as distinct but not as distinct from perception.

102. To introspection, the content of thought appears distinct from thought though it does not appear to be *given* as distinct. Feeling, so far as we are aware of thought as only symbolizing it, may be said to have a content, an unthought or unmeant content which, however, appears to introspection as only distinct in itself and not as distinct *from* feeling. While again in the case of thought or other psychic fact, introspection seeks to distinguish it from its content, it seeks to distinguish the unmeant content of feeling from the feeling and not *reversely*, though the seeking to distinguish does not amount to the knowledge of distinction in any case. Because psychic fact is distinguished in introspection from its object, it is believed to exist also outside introspection. But as the feeling is not thus distinguished from its content, it cannot be believed to exist outside introspection as a merely conscious fact. Feeling is never outside introspection, just as perception is never within introspection.

103. Introspection into feeling, however, is an awareness of the feeling as apparently distinct from the awareness. Introspection into psychic fact is a distinguishing of the fact which appeared undistinguished from itself, consciousness being implicitly self-consciousness in this sense. Introspection into feeling, however, is an *identifying* of the feeling which appeared to be outside introspection as a psychic fact illusorily bound up with a presentation and implies the annulment of this illusion. Feeling is bound up with thought and imagination, being the awareness of their detachment as presentation from their objects, corresponding to the known distinction of the objects from their presentation. In introspection into psychic fact, the felt detachment is symbolized as a thinkable distinction of the psychic fact from its object, though its merely symbolic character is not appreciated as such. In introspection into feeling, the distinction of feeling from its presentative content is appreciated as definitely not known

but only felt and symbolized. The content as presented is recognized to be not *its* content. To distinguish a feeling from the meant content is to view the content as a mere symbolism. When thought views the image as its symbol, the symbol still stands as presentation though it is not meant. But when along with feeling, there is the awareness of meaning as its symbol, the symbol is not only not felt: its object-reference lapses altogether. The meaning loses its actuality and turns into the form of a possible meaning. Possible meaning is no presentation, as the awareness *"as though feeling meant something"* is no belief in it as fact. There may be a faith that some meaning of feeling will emerge but the faith is not a belief in what is, at least, partly meant actually. It may imply a trying to think which is not so much a doing as a wishing, being but the free self-expressive play of the feeling. When a presentation is reduced to mere play, there is a make-believe and no belief. Not that the faith must be there but the belief in the object must lapse. Feeling as detached from meaning is awareness of the meaning as its symbolism and may in this sense be taken as implicitly introspective, being never a merely conscious fact outside introspection. Explicit introspection into feeling means only outgrowing the necessity of thus symbolizing feeling by meaning and recognizing that feeling does not mean anything but itself.

104. The place of willing may be indicated here as coordinate with feeling. If feeling represents the complete dissociation from objectivity, willing means the free identification with objectivity. Throughout we have been tracing the movement of dissociation, beginning with the dissociation of the perceived body from the object. To knowledge, the object is *there* and the body *here* is its presupposition; and as knowledge deepens, there is a regress to prior presuppositions, the felt body, et cetera, up to feeling or what we have called the knowledge of the merely unknown. Each presupposition persists undistinguished in a lower stage and hence feeling may be said to inform even the perceived object, though this is known only when feeling has been dissociated from thought. It is at this stage also that the identification in the lower stages is known to have been free in the sense of not being necessitated by the object. The playful self-expression of feeling in a meaning or thought as its symbol is the first conscious

identification with a lower stage, self-objectification without the lapse of dissociation, the initial act of objective willing as distinct from spiritual willing. Willing starts as the aesthetic expression of feeling. The freedom from thought is as much a progress as a regress, as much a willing as a feeling. Regress and progress are two distinct movements in the lower stages, distinct because the object as known is there the starting point. With the cancellation of the objective attitude, there is the consciousness of being free, of being unrestricted by the object whether for withdrawal from it in feeling or for conquest over it in willing.

105. Knowing means freedom both from blindness and from error, escape from the confusion of the object with the subject and from the identification of the subject with the object. As we have shown at many points, the distinguishing of the object from its presentation implies a half detachment of the presentation from the object when a consciousness emerges of something in the object that is unknown, the presentation being however not denied to be object. The consciousness of the unknown is at the stage we have reached understood as feeling inwardness; and the consciousness of the presentation as a ghostly object, as what cannot be denied as object but cannot, therefore, be asserted as such is now interpreted as the objectifying or self-externalizing function of the will. The so-called knowledge of the object thus appears to be a single function of inwardizing and objectifying, of regress and progress, of feeling and willing. The freedom or detachment implied in knowing means the outgrowing of the positive attitude of not knowing, of conscious entertainment of the unknown—which is feeling—and of *conscious* projection of objectivity—which is willing. Thus to the knowing attitude, feeling and willing appear as what are jointly outgrown and as what also symbolize the inwardness and reality of knowledge.

106. The positive consciousness of detachment from meaning which is the last residuum of the object is feeling. Feeling is the knowledge of the purely unknown as such, the unknown that is not even meant. It is only symbolized as knowledge *of* the unknown, though the unknown being unmeant, the preposition *of* has no meaning and is recognized as a mere exigency of language. There is no distinguishing of the knowledge from its

content: the knowledge stands by itself and is the awareness of its content as no content, as unmeant. The next stage would be the awareness of the content as unmeanable. In feeling there is still the demand for a symbolical meaning to be denied, a will to expression, the awareness of the absence of actual meaning and the non-denial of a possible meaning. That will to expression is a trying to think and there may come after the trial the consciousness of a failure to think and the consequent abandonment of the trial. Such consciousness of failure may be regarded as feeling that has purged itself from the persisting will to objectification, as the awareness not merely of the unknown but of the contradictory or unmeanable, of what is not imaginary but is given as false. It is feeling in the sense that it *comes*: if trying to think is still an activity, the consciousness of inability to think is what is borne in upon us.

107. The consciousness of given falsity or objective illusion has to be distinguished from the consciousness of the imaginary. In the example of the illusory snake corrected into the perceived rope, the snake appears after correction to have been not merely a sport of the imagination like golden mountain but to have been believed as real. At the same time while the disbelief in golden mountain implies no uncertainty as to its being merely imagined, the present disbelief in the snake implies an uncertainty as to its having been perceived. What we are conscious of now is that it is *as though* it was perceived. So we say about a dreamed object—"it is as though it was seen." The snake, we say now, was believed and not merely imagined but not known. What is now remembered as having been believed and appears as though it was known was not, therefore, merely imagined. Belief in an object ideated, as a psychic fact existing outside introspection, is presentation. The present awareness of an object as though it was known might be called appearance of presentation. The appearance of presentation is a disbelieved possibility of object. It cannot, however, be taken as imaginary, for an imaginary thing does not appear presented (with belief) at all. The awareness of an imagined thing may not be a belief in the thing but is belief in the presentation. The awareness of an imaginary thing is disbelief in the thing and is no belief in the presentation. The awareness of a

thing as illusory is not only disbelief in the thing but implies, at least, a positive doubt about its presentation. Disbelief in the imaginary thing may still be called knowledge, knowledge of the negation of all objective facthood. But disbelief in the illusory thing is not even knowledge of such negation, being the consciousness of an indetermination which is neither factual nor imaginary, neither presented with belief nor not presented at all. What being first presented with belief comes to be disbelieved cannot be asserted to be presented without belief: that it is presented cannot only be denied. Disbelief in the illusory object is not *knowledge* of its falsity but the awareness of what cannot be asserted or denied to be true. When this "indescribable" content is altogether rejected, there is knowledge not of falsity but of the self.

108. The indescribable is unmeanable and so there may be a consciousness of the unmeanable and not merely of the unmeant in feeling. This consciousness cannot be said to be not feeling, though there is no longer the belief in the possibility of symbolizing it by a meaning. Introspection into the first stage of the feeling process means, as has been shown, not a distinguishing of the feeling from thought—for feeling does not exist except in being thus distinguished—but an identification of it, the positive assertion of the feeling being itself only, of freedom from thought constituting the very being of feeling. Such freedom is a positive being because there is no rejection yet of *possible* thought or meaning. The awareness of the unmeanable then, as implying such rejection, is freedom from the being of feeling, though as the lapse of the trying to think *comes* as a result of such trying, it cannot be said to be not felt. Roughly then two stages of feeling can be distinguished—freedom from actual thought and freedom from possible thought, from the faith in a possible meaning, from the will to think. It is the persisting will to think that constitutes the being of feeling in the lower stage. Freedom from the will to think is thus feeling that has no being, possible feeling that yet is possible not to a will or trying but to feeling itself, being the feeling of self-negation as distinct from the lower feeling which is feeling of self-being.

109. The feeling of not having a feeling is not an uncommon

experience. The awareness of wanting a feeling—whether sense-enjoyment, aesthetic satisfaction, or spiritual serenity—is itself a feeling. All desire involves a present feeling of not having a feeling, an awareness of the "inferiority" of the anticipatory pleasure to the actual feeling that is to come. It is not simply one feeling *due* to the want of another feeling but the feeling of the want of its own being or actuality. Nor is it yet the disinterested awareness of the want, a detachment from it such as introspection would imply. It can only be characterized as the *feeling* of a feeling, with which are bound up interesting spiritual attitudes like sentimentalism on the one hand which confuses the felt want with the actual feeling that is wanted and the experience of the want on the other as a pain that miraculously ends in a fulfillment.

110. This feeling of a feeling is not introspection but the stage prior to it, even as the trying to think is prior to feeling. It is the negative of which introspection is the positive equivalent—the self-negation of feeling or feeling detached from its being. Such detachment or self-negation is already the attitude of knowledge, knowledge of what is neither felt nor unfelt, of a negation that cannot be denied, of the indeterminate unmeanable or indescribable. Such knowledge may be regarded as introspection that yet has a being and is not denied to be the object of introspection. Introspection proper is not the object of further introspection.

111. The nature of this pre-introspective knowledge may be intelligible through the analysis of a puzzle about the unmeanable. *Unmeanable* is itself a significant word and so the unmeanable, it may be said, is meant. The puzzle suggests a two-fold function of the significant word. Speaking as to the speaker has to be distinguished from speaking as to the hearer; and to the speaker himself, the word being spoken has a function different from the word as already spoken. What the speaker means as unmeanable after having tried to mean may be to the hearer what he does not even try to mean. Again, while in speaking of the unmeanable, as in any act of speaking, the speaker only means without contemplating the meaning as accomplished, the word as spoken appears either to his or to the hearer's contemplation to have an accomplished meaning. If the

speaker does not contemplate it, the hearer (or he himself later) may contemplate it; and if the speaker contemplates, the hearer may not. There is thus a difference between the meaning being coined out or being understood and the meaning as accomplished and contemplated. We are aware of the unmeanable in two stages, as the meant unmeanable and as the mere function of meaning or speaking. The knowledge implied in the former is of a contradiction while that implied in the latter is not *of* anything, being merely knowing. The feeling of feeling is the former kind of awareness while the latter is just introspection. Self-negation in feeling of feeling is still a felt being, existent knowledge rather than the function of knowing. Introspection is complete dissociation from felt being and is the pure knowing function.

Chapter 8
Spiritual Subjectivity (Cont.)

Introspection

112. Introspection into a subjective fact means a distinguishing of it. There is no direct introspective awareness of perceptual knowledge. In non-perceptual knowledge, object is already distinguished from presentation and the introspective awareness of such knowledge is the awareness of its distinction in itself with a feeling of its dissociation from the object. This feeling is symbolized as a thinkable distinction from the object by a reversal of the known distinction of the object from the presentation. Introspective distinguishing is only the knowledge of a subjective fact as distinct in itself, though in the case of subjective fact lower than feeling, it appears through such symbolized feeling of dissociation as the knowledge of the fact as distinct *from the object*. Feeling is nothing but this conscious dissociation, as is realized when presentation in the attenuated form of meaning is known to be distinct from feeling. Introspection into feeling from which meaning is known to be distinct—feeling which is nothing but the conscious dissociation from the object—is the awareness of feeling being distinct in itself only and does not involve the further symbolism of being distinct *from* anything. Thus while the introspective awareness of a psychic fact is the awareness of its distinc-

tion from object and, therefore, of its distinction in itself also as existing apart from introspection as presentation, the introspective awareness of a feeling proper is the knowledge of its distinction in itself only and is the recognition of the distinction as being entirely through introspection. Such recognition may be called an identification.

113. Introspection into feeling is the recognition of the distinct being of the feeling as entirely through the introspection. It is just the function of meaning the feeling, of distinguishing, referring to or speaking of the feeling. Meaning as a function as distinct from the meant is intelligible only after the self-negation of feeling, feeling of wanting a feeling, the detachment of feeling from its being or the awareness of the meant unmeanable. To mean not merely the conscious absence but the conscious impossibility of meaning is the pure function of subjectivity, the function of introspection that is not objective even in the form of the meant unmeanable. If the feeling of feeling is already a detachment from subjective being, it is as a contradiction, as a be-ënt want of feeling. Introspection is a subjectivity that is detached both from being and from negation, being positive as *freedom*. It is not simply like the meant unmeanable or the "indescribable" what is neither be-ënt nor non-be-ënt, a negation that cannot be asserted or denied. It is the positive of which the negation is not even tried to be meant. The negation of the function of meaning is a gratuitous problem in meaning which there is no call to solve. Unlike the illusory object which is first presented and then reduced to the unmeanable, this negation is an imaginary problem in meaning which can, indeed, always be asked in logical sport but suggests no actual uncertainty about the introspective function. The imaginary problem is never ousted but never amounts to an uncertainty about any actual belief. Introspection is an actual believing which can only be sought to be impugned by the imaginary problem of conceiving its negation and is, therefore, never actually impugned. The content believed in introspection is, as will appear presently, capable of being impugned but not the believing itself. We speak only of introspective believing because a belief the object of which turns out false is no longer a belief in the object but is still a fact to introspective memory as the

past believing in an unmeanable, as a contentless believing that is not other than the introspection.

114. The old argument against absolute skepticism that it is doubting on the strength of believing is untenable if it is intended to exclude doubt about the *object* of belief. The object of belief is always impugnable though the grounds of the doubt must be actual or believed to constitute a relevant doubt. The argument, however, is valid if it intends to say that believing cannot be doubted. It will be presently apparent that not object only but every subjective fact that is introspectively believed, even though it be meant as unmeanable, is capable of being doubted. Believing then would not be fact at all, being not even meant as unmeanable. Nor is it, therefore, an illusion, for an illusion about the subjective has a place, as will be shown, beyond the introspection that we are now considering.

115. Introspection is the function of believing or meaning which is not itself meant even as the unmeanable and is, therefore, not actually doubtable. It is just the first person I, the speaker who is not an object to introspection but is simply the function of speaking. Introspection is not believing *in* the I: it is the I, the believing that is not fact at all but is not, therefore, illusory. As not believing even in the meant unmeanable, it is not believing in anything distinguished from it and so may be loosely expressed as believing in itself. The conscious inadequacy of the expression is itself evidence of the believing being not believing *in* anything.

116. Introspection as a conscious dissociation even from feeling that is distinct only through it is an annulment of the distinction—what we have called identification. Introspection into a psychic fact bound up with presentation reveals that its subjective facthood is nothing but the facthood of feeling. Such introspection appears to be a believing in a distinct because the distinctness of psychic fact is not immediately annulled by introspection, being reduced in the first instance to the distinctness of feeling. The direct unidentifiability of the psychic fact is what constitutes its apparently independent being; and it is thus that the psychic fact is pronounced by introspection itself as having a ghostly existence outside introspection. That it is directly uniden-

tifiable is due to the fact that it is never a complete detachment from the felt body and that accordingly psychic fact never appears to it as having only the facthood of feeling. But there is the conscious semi-detachment of feeling from the meanable psychic fact pointing to the possibility of complete detachment; and there is the identifying introspection into feeling implying possible detachment from the being of feeling. This possible detachment from all distinct being is introspective awareness. Introspection is essentially the annulment of all distinct being, being self-identification or the conscious identity without being of the self.

117. The self is taken by Kant as the thinking function. The thinking function is thinking of a thought or accomplished meaning and Kant does not deny that the self as an Idea of the Reason is an accomplished meaning. There is, however, the awareness not only of trying to think without any accomplished meaning but also of the impossibility of meaning. We can mean the unmeanable and thus the speaking or meaning function is more fundamental than thinking. In calling introspection the self, we not only bespeak the detachment of the self from thinking and feeling but also take it to be a believing or self-identifying, the negation of which is not even a meant unmeanable and which, therefore, cannot be denied to be a self-knowing. The introspective self is self-knowing, not as having the self as the object of knowledge but as denying the distinct being of feeling, as identifying it without denying its being and as having itself no deniable being.

118. The self is the first person I. The *I* is not unmeanable nor is it meant—meant even as unmeanable. It is not unmeanable in the sense that it presents no problem in meaning at all and can be said to be neither meanable nor unmeanable. Meaning is the thinnest presentation of the object, as existing apart from introspection. *I* has no meaning in this sense: it has not even the meaning of being unmeant or unmeanable, which feeling in its two stages may be supposed to have. The word *I* is used by the speaker not for what is distinct but for what is only being distinguished by him; and it is not understood by the hearer to *mean* a distinct content. No two persons would use the word *I* of the same thing; but the speaker and the hearer must be agreed about a meaning. Yet if a person

understands me when I call myself *I*, though he does not use the word himself about me, it is—it may be contended—because of the meaning of the word. But in that case it would be a kind of general term meaning any speaker, in which sense, however, it is not used, not being applied to more than one thing at a time. The term, in fact, is not singular in the sense that different people use it of the same thing and not general in the sense that it is *understood* by any of the different things at a time. If a person using the word *I* is understood as referring to himself by another, it is not because the latter means the speaker by the word and would use the word to refer to the speaker. Thus it may be said that a speaker calling himself *I* is understood through the word but not through the meaning of the word. The word here has a meaning function but not a meaning: it is the expression of introspection or what may be called the *I*-function.

119. Like the word *unmeanable*, the word *I* illustrates a use of language other than for purposes of thinking, the former being still the expression of an inability to think while the latter has not even this negative reference to thought. The meaning function of the word *I* is to the speaker his actual introspection but the understanding of the word by the hearer is indicative of a form of consciousness subtler than introspection. It is the awareness of how the speaker would introspect, awareness of a possible introspection.

Chapter 9
Spiritual Subjectivity (Cont.)

Beyond Introspection

120. The realization of what a speaker means by the word *I* is the hearer's awareness of a possible introspection. Such awareness is as much knowledge as actual introspection. The speaker calls himself *I* and may be understood by the hearer as *you*. As thus understood, the introspective self is individual, not an individual being—for introspection is not a subjective *being* like feeling—but the function of addressing to another self. The speaker does not understand himself through the meaning of the word *I*: his introspection is through the word and not through its meaning and is less a self-knowing than a self-revealing, revealing to a possible understander of the word *I*. Yet as the addressing attitude is only implicit, it is to him accidental and posterior to his self-knowing. To the understanding self however, although he understands the speaker's self-knowing because he is himself self-knowing, his understanding of the other *I* is primary while his own self-knowing is accidental and secondary. The speaker knows himself in implicitly revealing to the hearer and the hearer knows the speaker in implicitly knowing himself. Neither self-knowing nor other-knowing is through thinking or the meaning of the word and both might be called "intuition" in

this negative sense. There are thus two cases—self-intuition with other-intuition implicit in it and other-intuition with self-intuition implicit in it. Both are actual knowledge, implying the use other than the thinking use of a word like *I*, which is like a pointing gesture at once self-evidencing and self-evident. My self-consciousness is not the understanding of the meaning of the word *I*: the word only reveals it to another. His understanding of the word as referring to me is not the understanding of it in the sense he would use it himself. The word has no meaning either to him or to me and yet it stands like any other word for the same thing to both. This *standing for* is not only not meaning but not also mere symbolizing. It is on the one hand revealing and on the other an accomplished revelation, at once self-evidencing and self-evident. The word may be said at once to symbolize and to be symbolized by my introspective self. The hearer takes it to symbolize myself but I, the speaker, symbolize it by myself or in a sense explained before, incarnate myself in it. The reference of the word *I* varies with the user of it: its meaning function is through his self-consciousness, is symbolized by his meaning function which is what he is primarily aware of, the symbol being better known than what is symbolized by it. Because the word *I* is at once the symbol and the symbolized, it cannot be said to have simply the symbolizing function. It is this characteristic value of a word other than the meaning value or merely symbolizing value that indicates a grade of self-consciousness higher than our actual introspection.

121. Actual introspection is implicitly social, being a speaking or addressing or self-evidencing to another possible introspection or self to which its conscious solitariness or self-identity is evident. The evidencing and the evidentness are actual to different selves, speaker or hearer. The evidentness as to the hearer is, however, only a possible evidentness to the speaker. Actual introspection is unrealized knowledge because it is actually only self-evidencing to another and not self-evident to itself. One's own self should be self-evident, should be intuited by oneself even as it is intuited by another. The introspection that is actually reached by the annulment of the alien character of feeling as

subjective being is, as already shown, only a speaking, self-evidencing or self-revealing, a function in the Kantian sense though not thinking function, a kind of transcendental willing which is not known by the introspector but should be known as it is already known by another self. The self should be at once self-evidencing and self-evident but so far we have only the self as self-evidencing and evident to another.

122. The other self is to the self-evidencing self a possible introspector whose intuition of the latter again is a possible intuition to the latter. It is because the actual introspector is thus aware of the possible introspector that he can conceive a possible introspection of his own beyond his actual introspection; and it is only as he is thus aware of a possibly intuited subjectivity that he can understand the possibility of a subjective illusion. The awareness of these possibles in oneself—possible knowledge and possible illusion of subjectivity—indicates the necessity of a spiritual discipline of realization, realization of the knowledge of the self already implied by introspection.

123. Introspection into a possible or non-existent mental state is or involves understanding of a word meaning the mental state. To mean a mental state is not to think it: it is either to feel the want of it or to give it a distinction which it has not, which is like creating it. Where the mental state is not present, to mean it is to remember it, to want it or to dreamily wish it. All these are forms of awareness of a possible mental state and may be regarded as a stage of introspection prior to the introspection into an actual mental state. If it is introspection, it cannot be said to be completely dissociated yet from subjective being and as such it is capable of being itself introspected into. There can be, for example, introspection into the conscious want of a feeling.

124. The want of a feeling is an actual feeling and introspection into it, as into any feeling, means its identification with the introspection. It does not, however, mean identification with itself of the feeling that is wanted. The introspector is not aware of such a feeling as his feeling: the possible feeling is an unappropriated feeling. The introspective awareness of an unappropriated subjective state is like the awareness of another self having it. To

the introspector it is the awareness of what he himself *might* appropriate. There may be actual knowledge, as immediate as introspection and standing on a level with it, of another self and his subjective state. But as the introspector only imagines and does not know his own being, his awareness of his possible subjective state is not actual knowledge. Introspection into the awareness of a possible subjective state is thus possible or imaginary introspection. Such introspection is half dissociated from the actually introspective self, half dissociated in the sense that we only cannot deny it to be *our* introspection. It is, indeed, completely dissociated from the possible subjective state but not from the actual awareness of it. Complete dissociation from this actual awareness is reached when the content of it is a subjective state that is illusory and not merely absent or possible.

125. There are illusions about the subjective just as there are illusions about the objective. A subjective state appears illusory to later introspection into the subjective state that supersedes it through, it may be, the effervescence of interest or other subtle subjective cause. But a simple form of subjective illusion may be presented in connection with an objective illusion. When the objective presentation with which a psychic fact is bound up turns out to be illusory, there is at least a partial reduction of the psychic fact to illusion. In the example of the correction of the presentation of snake into the presentation of *this* rope, the fear as of *that* snake—that individual fear—is, as pointed out before, also felt to be, if not illusory, at least incapable of being asserted as a past fact. We cannot say that we feared *that* snake if we now know that the snake never was. Some feeling bound up with the bodily reaction was, indeed, felt but *that* feeling of fear or fear of *that* snake was never felt. The specific character of the feeling bound up with the past belief in the snake cannot be said to have existed. Introspection now not only does not identify *that* feeling with itself: it rejects it as what it cannot possibly appropriate. There is a doubt, if not a denial, of possible appropriation of it by any individual self, of its being knowable by any introspection and yet it is introspection itself that denies the possibility.

126. Introspection is the awareness of a subjective fact as owing

its facthood to itself and is in this sense the identification or appropriation of it. Such subjective fact may be itself the awareness of the absence or possibility of another subjective fact and introspection into it is the awareness of this other fact as not actually appropriated but as possibly appropriated by another introspection. The subjective fact introspected into may be again the awareness of the impossibility of a subjective mode previously taken to be fact. Introspection here would be the awareness of this mode as beyond all possible introspective appropriation. One gets here the hint of an introspection that is not appropriative, of the appropriative function being accidental to the introspective self, of the distinctness or exclusiveness of *I* being an eliminable feature, of an intuitable self-identity that has not any subjective fact distinct from it to identify. Introspection that is not appropriation would be self-intuition, the *I* that is evident to itself and not merely to another, that does not like the individual *I* create a distinct subjective mode by distinguishing to resume it by identifying and proclaim this resumption again by speaking in the first person to another possible person. The possibility of such a silent self-enjoying *I* is intelligible only because we are aware of certain subjective modes previously appropriated as not only now unappropriated but as utterly unappropriable and as accordingly appearing only *as though* they were distinct. The absolute intuitable self is only understood if the non-being of distinction is understood. Objective illusion is still a meant unmeanable, meant and therefore distinguished. But subjective illusion is not even meant as unmeanable. Introspection too is an unmeant meaning function; it is not known as distinct nor is it primarily so much a distinguishing as an identifying so far as it is knowledge. It is, however, still a distinguishing in the act of self-revealing and therefore also a distinguishing from itself as possible. The awareness of subjective illusion goes beyond introspection, being the explicit awareness of illusorily distinguishing, of *creating* a distinction that is no fact at all. The non-being of distinction is finally understood here and hence too the conception of the absolute self.

Chapter 10
The Subject as Freedom

127. The subject is understood as what intends by the word *I*. The subject that intends is other than the subject that understands, being self-evident as self-evidencing to another and not to itself. The intuited subject is not only revealed but revealing: it is directly known as self-expressing in the spoken word *I* without being meant by it. It does not, however, intuit itself, as the intuiting subject also does not reveal itself. There is no introspective awareness of being revealed or incarnated in the word *I*, of one's freedom to self-expression as itself an evident fact. There is at best an imaginative demand for such awareness, for the realization of the felt identification with the word (or the object) as presupposing dissociation from it, for the transformation of the felt freedom into the intuition of freedom. It is in introspection that we are aware of this demand for the consummation of the freedom that is felt in every grade of subjectivity in respect of the object presented to it. The object appears alien to the subject up to the stage of thought. The feeling subject is free from the thought or meant content insofar as the latter is reduced to a symbolism. But it is still subject having being, subject that can still be object to introspection, being free but not freedom itself. The introspective

subject is, indeed, free from this being or possible objectivity and is thus freedom itself but it is still a distinct individual though only unconsciously. It knows itself not as *itself* but as a distinct subject that is only possibly identical with itself. It is thus aware of a demand to know this subject as actually itself, to annul its possible distinction from itself and, therefore, also its actual distinctness through the word *I*. The demand is for the intuition of the subject as absolute freedom.

128. The introspective self is aware of itself as the psychic self and the bodily self. At all stages it knows itself as to be known. It knows the bodily self indeed as known not only as object but also as definitely separated from other objects. But it does not know it like other objects as having a space-position and is aware of the demand to realize its positionless objectivity. The psychic self is also known as identified with objectivity as pure form or pure meaning but it is only felt as dissociated from the perceived body; and in introspection we are aware of the demand to realize this felt dissociation in knowledge. The introspective self is unaware of being objective to itself though it understands another self calling itself *I* and thus knows it as having objective distinctness, the distinctness of the word *I*. As, however, itself revealing through the word to another self, it is aware of itself as a possibly understood distinct entity. It knows itself not as known like the psychic or bodily self but as only to be known. As to be known, it is understood as what is only symbolized as distinct like the word *I* and what would lose its distinctness in being actually known. The subject is understood as freedom that is real and is characterizable by no objective category, not even by the category of distinctness. As we do not in introspection cease to be the bodily self which alone is actually evident to us, the subject that is absolutely unobjective or is freedom itself is to us only a possibility to be realized. The idea of realizing the subject arises only because we are actually identified with the body while we are introspectively aware of ourselves as not objective and yet as definitely positive. Introspective awareness of oneself is awareness of the subject as not only not objective in the sense of being thought or meant but also as what cannot be said to have the being of feeling nor to be contradictory like the feeling of the want

of a feeling nor even to be distinct like the subject to which it reveals itself. At the same time it is not awareness of a mere negation or of an indefinite. This definite positive cannot be said to be not known, though as actually undissociated from the object we cannot assert it to be known. We are only aware of not being dissociated, being dissociated to the extent implied by such awareness. Such implied dissociation is possible freedom that is to be realized as evident.

129. The consciousness of not being actually dissociated is present even in the stage of bodily subjectivity where alone actual dissociation is known in some measure and not merely felt as in higher stages. It is known, as has been pointed out, as the perceived separation in space of the body from the outside object, though there is a feeling still of one's body not being perceived in a space-position, all position being relative to it. In higher stages, there is no knowledge of freedom from the object but only a feeling of it, the feeling so far as it falls short of knowledge being the implicit awareness of not being actually free from the object. The higher the stage of subjectivity, the less is the freedom felt to be achieved though the more assured is the faith in its achievability. In the introspective stage, the feeling of achieved freedom lapses altogether, since it is here that the possibility of freedom is first definitely known. The faith in its achievability, however, is completely assured in this stage and takes the form of a conscious spiritual demand for the intuition of freedom as evident.

130. Three broad stages of subjectivity have been exhibited—the bodily, the psychical, and the spiritual. In the bodily stage, three substages have been discussed—the body as externally perceived, the body as internally perceived or felt, and the absence of object known as a present fact. As externally perceived, the bodily subject is the center of the perceived world but is not itself perceived as in it. As felt, it is definitely known to be not in this world though it is not known as not the externally perceived body. The subject that imaginatively perceives the absence of an object is also like the felt body not consciously dissociated from the perceived body but the subject that knows absence through conscious non-perception is consciously dis-

sociated from it. He feels himself unlike the felt body as definitely without reference to space-position and as only the time-position—present or *now*, as distinct from the image of the absent object, which also is without this reference but is not consciously felt as *now*.

131. The image of the object whose absence is known in conscious non-perception marks the transition to the psychic stage. It appears as the object that is absent and is not yet felt to be dissociated from it. The psychic stage begins when attention is shifted from the objective fact of absence to the image. As attended to, the image appears as imaging or the forming of a form, the process and the product being presented at once. The consciousness of the form as evident in the forming process and as a product that does not yet come in time *after* it is the idea as undissociated from the image. A later stage is the idea as dissociated from the image, or pictorial thought which wants to be imaged and is definite so far as it is imaged. Non-pictorial thought comes next, thought that is definite in itself and has properly no image though an image may serve as its metaphor or symbol. These grades of image and thought are the grades of presentation which is explicitly felt to be dissociated from the object. Such dissociated presentation is known in introspection to have no space-position and is at least not known to have time-position. The image still appears, however, as though it had spatial form and to be forming as though it were a temporal process. Some trace of this quasi-temporal process may persist in thought but thought as a non-pictorial meaning is felt to be free from it and to be eternally complete. Still such meaning appears as though it were object, being introspectively believed like other psychical facts to exist outside introspection. Its presentational character is explicitly indicated by the consciousness of the absence of accomplished meaning in what we have called *trying* to think which may be taken as pointing to the positive freedom from objective meaning such as characterizes the non-presentational or spiritual stage of subjectivity.

132. The positive freedom from objectivity appears in the first instance as feeling. Feeling still seems to mean something but the

meaning here so far as it is formulated is avowedly a symbolism for it only. To introspection indeed, feeling appears to be object but not as what may exist outside introspection. Its alien character is to introspection only apparent, being distinct only through introspection and not capable of existing outside introspection except as illusorily bound up with a presentation. The feeling subject has a being to introspection so that it is free and is not freedom itself. The next stage is the feeling of wanting a feeling, which is, in fact, a felt contradiction or self-negation that still appears distinct from the introspection into it. The introspecting subject, however, is not introspected into and is self-revealing through the word *I*. It is aware of being revealed or evident not to itself but to the subject addressed and therefore of being *possibly* revealed to itself also. As thus only possibly evident to itself, it is unappropriated by itself while as introspecting, it is aware of addressing a subject and of being dissociated from it by the very fact of addressing. It thus feels being distinct but does not know itself as distinct. It is aware of the subject as possibly free from distinctness, as its very self but not as exclusively its own.

133. I am introspectively conscious of my body as subject but not as not mine or the appropriated. I am conscious of a psychic fact as not mine, as subject that is not, however, not *me* as the known. As, however, I speak of *I* in introspection, I intend what before I spoke was not *me* but not what was not a distinct *I*. There is no introspection into introspection but just as perception is known indirectly in introspection into some other subjective state like memory, so introspection is known indirectly in introspection into feeling. Feeling appears to introspection as subject that has no reference to object, as I but still as I distinct from I, as the be-ënt I illusorily distinct from the introspective I. Introspection into the feeling I then is awareness of the introspecting I as not distinguished but as only distinguished *from*, as that from which being and non-being are both distinguished, as that which cannot be denied to be distinct in itself but of which such distinction is not known.

134. The apprehension of I as not even distinct in itself is indicated by the consciousness of subjective illusion, of a mode of subjectivity that is not only unappropriated but unappropriable. There is occasion to correct the conceit not only of *my* body and of *me* as a presentation, not only of I as felt being but also of I as an

actual distinct introspector. The introspecting self that I am indirectly aware of in introspection into feeling appears to be an actual self. In introspection into the feeling of wanting a feeling it turns out to be only a possible self that is still distinct as an introspector. But there may be the consciousness of a feeling being illusorily wanted: I may, for example, recognize not only that I am not religious but also that even my hankering after religion is not real but only a sentimental make-believe. Such recognition would be the awareness not only of an unappropriated but of an unappropriable religious aspiration, of the self that only appears as I aspiring and *is not it*, is not an actual introspector and not even a possible introspector.

135. I am never positively conscious of my present individuality, being conscious of it only as what is or can be outgrown, only as I feel freeing myself from it and am free to the extent implied by such feeling. I do not know myself as free but I conceive that I can be free successively as body from the perceived object, as presentation from the body, as feeling from presentation and as introspective function from feeling. I am not introspectively aware of my actual introspective individuality but I am aware in my introspection into feeling that the self from which the feeling is distinguished may not actually introspect and may not even possibly introspect, that individual as it is as introspecting—individual or distinct freedom without being, it may be free even from this distinctness, may be freedom itself that is de-individualized but not therefore indefinite—absolute freedom that is to be evident.

*The Concept
of the Absolute and Its
Alternative Forms*

sciousness of a relation prior to reflection, the relation of contents may be said to be prior to the relation of content and consciousness in the sense that the former is intelligible by itself while the latter is intelligible only in terms of the former.

3. There are those who hold that because we are only reflectively conscious of relation, the relation between content and consciousness should be read into the relation of content and content and not vice versa. The relation of content and consciousness is to them a transparent identity-in-difference and all relation of contents is to be understood as the same relation in an implicit form. The difficulty is that the relation of content and consciousness is not explicitly or self-evidently appreciated as an identity-in-difference by reflection itself, being, in fact, claimed to be so appreciated only in a higher consciousness called absolute or speculative consciousness. The possibility, however, of this supra-reflective consciousness may be disputed and it is necessary in the first instance to show if and how reflection itself points to it.

4. Prima facie to reflection, the relation of content and consciousness appears as an implicative distinction. We are reflectively aware of the content as distinct from and in necessary reference to consciousness and the reference is not merely verbal but is implicitly an assertion. In the case of an asserted implication between two terms, the fact asserted is a relation (or unity), the terms of which are not the terms asserted to be in implication. If A is asserted to imply B, a factual relation is meant but A is not understood as a term of the relation. A here stands for a fact which need not have the relation but is thought as having it, the fact being not altered by being so thought. This fact should be capable of being expressed by a term that does not refer to the relation and the relation should be taken as between this term and the implied term B. For every implying term, it is necessary to find such a non-implying term, if possible; and until and unless it is found, the implication has to be taken as an *indefinite* formulation of a factual relation (or unity). To reflective consciousness there is implication between the content and the consciousness of it and the implication points to a factual relation (or unity) of which one of them at least is not really a term. One of them at least stands for an unnamed something which need not be related to the other. Some factual relation then appears to be only *indefinitely* formulated as the implication of content and con-

The Concept of the Absolute and Alternative Forms

1. Philosophy starts in reflective consciousness. Refle
the awareness of a content *as to* a mode of consciousne
phrase "as to" means some relation and it is in reference
relation that the concept of the absolute has to be unde
What is this relation?

2. We ordinarily understand a relation as between the c
of consciousness and we have here apparently to conceiv
such relation as subsisting between content and conscio
Of the two relations—between content and content, and b
content and consciousness—the latter has to be unders
terms of the former. Not that we know relation in ol
consciousness before we come to be reflectively conscio
relation between content and consciousness. To be awa
relation *as such* between two terms, of their relation as
from their whole having the form of being, is to be awar
same time of the possibility of the terms being not related
relation. Now unlike a term known to be existent, a r
known to subsist between two terms cannot be *imagine*
absent. The possible absence of a known relation, in fa
never be apprehended in merely objective consciousness.
we can know a relation *as such* of two contents only in ref
which is specifically the consciousness of a relation be
content and consciousness. Yet although there can be r

sciousness in the reflective stage.

5. Now if it can be shown within reflection that this indefinite relation cannot be denied to be a distinction and cannot be denied also to be an identity, a stage of consciousness in which distinction and identity of the same terms are positively known together may be taken to be demanded by reflection which cannot understand them together. That the content is somehow distinct from consciousness is obvious to reflection but identity is not so obvious. What immediately appears is an indefinite distinction between content and consciousness: the terms are undoubtedly distinct but they are not wholly distinguishable. Have we the right to interpret this vague indistinguishability as an identity?

6. The indefinite relation of content and consciousness appears to reflection at once as distinction and as not distinction but this non-distinction cannot be positively asserted as an identity. Things may come to be distinguished that were undistinguished but what are once distinguished cannot be later taken to be non-distinct without at least one of the terms being taken to be illusory. Hence to distinguish terms imperfectly is to be able to assert their distinction but neither to assert nor to deny their identity.

7. But it may be contended that distinction and identity stand on the same footing in respect of undeniability: like distinction identity also once apprehended cannot be denied. That we distinguish what were undistinguished does not mean that we knew their *relation* of identity which is now denied. We reply that it is possible to deny the relation of identity even when it is explicitly apprehended. There is something peculiar about the relation of identity, as expressed in the dilemma: if its terms are not distinct, they are not related at all, and if they are distinct they are not identical. We cannot get rid of the dilemma and admit identity as a relation unless we hold that while the distinction of its terms is cognitively undenied, it is positively entertained only in non-cognitive consciousness. The fact A in the context M is said to be identical with A in the context N and A has the differential characters x and y in the contexts, which are presented and yet as neither factual nor non-factual. If the characters be facts, A cannot be identical in the two contexts and if they be no facts at all, there is no distinction of terms and, therefore, no relation. They have accordingly to be taken as not cognized

characters but aesthetically apprehended expressions which do not preclude the cognized identity of A and yet are themselves cognitively undenied. To assert a relation is not to *assert* a distinction between its terms but only not to deny it. We may be affectively or conatively aware of a distinction where we do not intellectually disbelieve the distinction but do not also assert it. Identity then such as is knowable is a relation of terms, the distinction of which is undenied but unknown. Now what is unknown and yet speakable as felt *may* come to be known. If the differential characters x and y come to be known, the identity of A would be denied. Identity cannot accordingly be taken to be undeniable like distinction.

8. The indefinite relation then of content and consciousness should not be interpreted as indefinite identity. There is no demand, therefore, in reflection for a stage of conscious in which content and consciousness may be explicitly seen to be identical in difference. The only necessary demand in knowledge is that what appears as indefinite in an assignable respect should be definable in that respect. If further the indefiniteness is such as *necessarily* appears to a stage of consciousness, that stage is taken to demand a higher stage where the indefinite gets defined. To reflection, the relation of content and consciousness appears necessarily as an indefinite distinction only and not as an indefinite identity. The demand is for this distinction to be defined and for a supra-reflective consciousness where this distinction can be visualized.

9. The concept of the absolute in any form is taken to belong to a supra-reflective consciousness. The possibility and nature of this consciousness have to be understood in reflection as a necessary problem. The conception of an explicit identity-in-difference of content and consciousness is not demanded in reflection. Reflection demands only a non-implicational distinction of them to define the necessarily implicational or indefinite distinction that is presented to it. The absolute accordingly has to be problematically understood within reflection as meaning not an identity but only a completely definite distinction of content and consciousness. It may be that the supra-reflective consciousness in which the reflective implication of content and consciousness is turned into a non-implicatory distinction is itself consciousness of identity in a symbolic or metaphorical sense. But in any case identity as *a logical relation* has to be definitely denied between content and consciousness before this mystic identity can be appreciated.

10. We are concerned for the present with the conception of the absolute such as is intelligible as a problem to reflection. We have to trace in detail how the indefinite distinction of content and consciousness can be defined, how their apparent identity can be denied, how, in fact, the implicatory distinction can be resolved into a non-implicatory distinction. We shall find presently that the implicatory distinction of content and consciousness varies according as the consciousness is knowing, feeling, or willing. The implication is resolvable in different ways in these three spheres and the absolute is understood in the reflective stage in terms of the mode of resolution in each case. Knowing, feeling and willing will then each have its own formulation of the absolute—namely, truth, value, and reality (or freedom) respectively, as will be justified later. In the reflective stage these absolutes or formulations of the absolute will be found to be un-unifiable and to be in a sort of alternation. Whether a mystical identity of the absolutes can be reached in the supra-reflective consciousness does not concern us. Our problem is to show how reflection demands a specific absolute in each case.

11. What is specifically apprehended in non-cognitive consciousness cannot be literally formulated in terms of knowledge. Philosophy which cognitively deals with the contents of all consciousness should claim to know *not* the non-cognitive contents themselves but only *that* they are non-cognitive, that we believe in contents which we do not know. It can, therefore, speak of these believed contents only by a sort of intellectual symbolism *as though* they were known. To reflection, the implicative distinction of content and consciousness varies according as the consciousness is knowing, feeling, or willing. The variations may be represented by three modes of distinction that we recognize as between known contents. If A is distinct from B, B may be simply an other, or it may be constitutive of A, or A and B may be both constitutive of C. So the content that is distinguished in reflection from consciousness may be spoken of as unconstituted by consciousness or as constituted by consciousness or as along with consciousness constituting some kind of unity. The first mode of distinction is the relation of content and consciousness in knowing and the last two will be found to appropriately symbolize the relation in willing and feeling respectively.

12. The content of a knowing act is unconstituted by the act. The *particular* act of knowing discovers and does not construct the

object known, even if the object be admitted to be constructed by *some* knowing. Knowledge would appear to mean that the object known is in some sense independent of it though it may be a question whether what we ordinarily claim to know is properly said to be known and to be independent of the knowing. Where the object is colored by the particularity of the act of knowing, it may be said to be only empirically known but it is still taken to be known so far as it is believed to be independent of it.

13. The content of willing may be said to be an act, an end, or the empirical embodiment of the end—the organization of certain objective facts (including the means) by the end. None of these is a fact that can be said to be known in the willing, believed as independent of the willing in the sense the content of knowing is independent of knowing. Each is constituted by willing in the sense that apart from willing it is nothing at all. It cannot be said that it is a future fact that is *known* in the willing. Willing is, indeed, some form of consciousness of the future but the future here, unlike the future that is said to be known, is not a fact but a contingency, not what *will* be but what *would* be *if* it were willed, not as already determined but what is being determined by the willing and as therefore apart from the willing nothing at all. Yet the content of willing is distinct from willing, distinct as what is constituted is distinct from what constitutes it.

14. Reflective knowing is consciousness of the known object as distinct from the knowing. Reflective willing is consciousness of the act willed as being distinguished by the willing from itself. Neither is consciousness primarily of the distinction itself or the distinguishing. Reflective feeling is primarily consciousness of the distinction (or the distinguishing) of content and consciousness. To be conscious of a content *as* felt is to be conscious of the content in unity with the feeling or of feeling unified with the content. The unity of two contents means—whatever else it means—an imperfect distinction between them; and we have to understand the unity of content and consciousness on this analogy. The unity of which reflective feeling is conscious is the imperfect distinction between content and consciousness, taken itself as a content. To be conscious of a content as known or willed is not even to be implicitly conscious of a unity of content and consciousness. The known content appears to reflection as perfectly distinct from knowing and a unity of perfect distincts cannot be reflectively conceived to be knowable. The content of

willing as constituted by the willing alone cannot be understood to constitute along with the willing any unity other than the content itself. It is only in reflective feeling that we are conscious of something, namely, value that is as much content as consciousness, that is not indeed *both* of them at once but what each of them is and is not alternately. The felt content is imperfectly distinguished from feeling but not constituted by it in the sense that apart from it, it is nothing at all. We do not, indeed, know but cannot deny that the value of an object is really in it.

15. Reflective consciousness is definite consciousness of something. The content of feeling of which we are reflectively conscious is not a definite content. What is perfectly distinct from another or constituted by another in the sense of being nothing without it is definite in itself. What, however, is imperfectly distinct from another and unconstituted by it is not definite in itself. Now an indefinite can only be referred to in connection with a definite content. What we are definitely conscious of in reflective feeling is the imperfect distinction itself of content and consciousness, this indefinite *as such* being, in fact, their unity. The indefinite content of feeling can only be referred to as a factor of this unity.

16. The content of knowing then is perfectly distinct from knowing and is unconstituted by it. The content of willing is imperfectly distinct from willing though distinct in itself and is constituted by it. Content and consciousness make a unity in the case of feeling but not in the case of knowing and willing. There are thus three modes of distinction of content and consciousness of which we are reflectively conscious. Each of these is an implicative or indefinite distinction in some sense and the indefiniteness will be found to consist in the fact that a relation that is intelligible as between content and content is only half intelligible when taken to be the relation between content and consciousness.

17. To begin with knowing. If the content of knowing be perfectly distinct from knowing, how can the distinction be implicative or indefinite at all? It is implicative in the sense that the content of knowing is *necessarily* understood in reflection as what is perfectly distinct from knowing. The content *implies* such a reference to knowing and apparently means nothing without it. When one content is asserted to imply another, a relation is asserted of which, as we said, the implying content is not really a *relatum* but some other content which need not have the relation

and which as thought with the relation is the implying content. This irrelative content may not be actually formulated but we conceive it to be formulable. It is difficult to conceive, however, what the known content apart from the knowledge-relation can possibly mean, since it is before the mind only as known.

18. The consciousness of a content as known is not, indeed, the consciousness of it as a fact necessarily related to knowing but it is not also the positive consciousness of it as only accidentally related to knowing. Reflection, in fact, on knowing tells us nothing about whether the content known is or is not necessarily known. The known content *means* indeed what is perfectly distinct from knowing but this verbal reference to knowing need not mean a *necessary factual* relation. The perfect distinction, too, does not mean that the content stands for something that would be even if it were not known by any one. Both the idealistic and the realistic positions here appear to be overstatements. In one sense, however, the realistic position may be said to have an advantage, for although reflection does not testify that what is known need not be known, it does not deny it while the idealistic view that the content is constituted by the knowing of it appears to be plainly opposed to reflective testimony.

19. It may be, however, that if and when the realistic conception of the known content as what need not be known is realized, the idealistic notion of its being constituted by knowing will be found to have a meaning. Criticism of knowledge may show that all that is actually taken to be known in the reflective stage is in some respect constituted by the particular act of knowing and, therefore, is in that respect not properly known though its known character cannot be denied altogether. Meantime we may reject the ordinary idealistic argument that to be aware of knowing an object is to be aware of recognizing it, aware therefore of the object as necessarily known. There is actually no consciousness of recognizing the object in the literal sense of remembering the past knowing of it. All that is actually meant is that to be aware of knowing an object is to be aware of knowing *truth*, knowing something—in other words—to be eternal or timeless. The object may be temporal but that it is in time is not itself a temporal fact. To know is to have a timeless truth revealed but this does not mean that it is timelessly *known* and so known *again* in the present act of knowing. There is apparently no ground to assume either a

previous knowing or of a timeless, impersonal, or universal knowing along with the present knowing to justify the use of the word "recognition."

20. The realistic position that the known content may exist unknown is not denied but cannot also be asserted in the reflective consciousness. It may be said, however, that it cannot be denied or asserted because only the proposition is meaningless. Can reflection understand it as a possibility? The possibility, we reply, is understood in reference to what we take to be *self-evidently* known. Certain known contents appear at least to be self-evident, not simply evident. So long as the evident is not contrasted with the self-evident, we say about it "it is" and not "it is *to me*." When it is contrasted however, we say "it is *to me*" (though not "to me only"), while of the self-evident we say simply "it is." To say "it is *to me*" is to suggest that it may not be; and to say—in denial of this possibility—that "it is" is to imply that it might not have been to the knower at all, that it is eternally true, that it is truth literally revealing itself. If anything then is known to be self-evident, it is known as what need not be known.

21. That the known content may exist—or more accurately—may be true without being known is then intelligible as a problem to reflection. It is, therefore, deniable, and it is not denied (though not asserted) because some content claimed to be self-evident appears to be implied in all knowledge. What is taken to be known is thus implicitly believed to be self-evident and only in this sense to be what need not be known. The realistic view of the independence of the known content, of its knownness being accidental, can only be admitted in the sense of the content being in some respect self-evident or self-revealing. The realist's definition of knowledge has to be accepted; but the question against him would be if what is claimed to be known is really known, is independent of the particular act of knowing or knowing generally. It is not the question if what is taken to be true is true. Value, for example, may be claimed to be known but it may be legitimately asked if it is known at all, if it is not merely believed in a non-cognitive way. So one may ask if what is taken by Kant to be only empirically known as involving construction of experiences is, as the realist will claim, really known, known as independent of the constructivity of the knowing act. The Kantian view may or may not be accepted but the question is certainly

legitimate if what is claimed to be known is known in the realist's sense of the term. The realist apparently would not admit the necessity of testing whether what is supposed in the first instance to be known is really known.

22. The known content should be what need not be known but where is the content that is known as such? The self-evident, we take it, is what is known to be independent of knowing in the sense of being eternally true without requiring to be known; but is anything admitted to be self-evident in the reflective consciousness? No known content is absolutely indubitable and in any case there is no agreement as to what content is indubitable. But some content or other appears self-evident in the sense of there being an explicit consciousness of doubt about it being unintelligible. The unintelligibility of doubt about a content should be distinguished from what is called the inconceivability of the opposite. Inconceivability of the opposite is understood only by trying to conceive it and to try to conceive it is to entertain a problem in thinking or meaning, if not of knowing. But there are cases where the problem of thinking the opposite of the content known is not entertained and one is conscious of its not arising at all. To be conscious of a content as self-evident is to be conscious not of its negation being unmeanable but of the problem of meaning the negation not even arising. We are conscious of the self-evident in this sense though the negation of what appears as such may later come to be conceived through a new self-evident cognition or revelation.

23. What we reflectively speak of as true or false is a judgment. The self-evident is that of which we cannot be conscious except as true. Is there then any self-evident judgment? To form a judgment is apparently always to be conscious of the *problem* of meaning its negation. This applies even to what is taken as a necessary judgment. Its negation is found to be inconceivable only after it has been tried to be conceived, and it is so found because it is but the elaboration of a systemic concept which is really a *postulate* that is neither true nor false and may admit of rival postulates. It is a direction of imagination in which what tends to be imagined is *eo ipso* believed. The belief is here not properly cognitive but is what may be roughly called a feeling of cognition. It is the consciousness that something *must be* without the consciousness that it is: it is as though one dimly felt what

must be. The so-called necessary judgment is an analysis of the content of such felt cognition and is not properly knowledge.

24. What however is inferred, that is, believed as what *must be* because something *is,* is believed also as what *is* and as such cannot be said to be merely felt as known. It is only the necessary that is not consciously inferred that should be so characterized. That a conclusion follows from a premise or premises is the only content that can be claimed in reflective consciousness as self-evidently known and not merely necessarily known, that is, felt to be known. Properly speaking, indeed, that a conclusion follows from a premise is not a judgment though expressed as such. The "following" is not a relation of contents that is itself a content coordinate with them. Still as it is not an arbitrary subjective relating of contents, we cannot say it is not a *believed* relation though it is not content of consciousness.

25. A disguised form of this inferential "following" we have in a judgment like "A implies B" which may be paraphrased "to know A is to know B." What does the word "is" here stand for? The two knowings stand for subjective acts but the connecting word "is" does not mean another act coordinate with them. Nor does it mean a relation of the contents A and B that is a third content. It appears to be a relation not of the contents but of the cognitions in respect of their content, being itself however no subjective act of cognition. It cannot be said not to be known though it is not content of the knowing of which A and B are contents. Whether it is the content of the reflective consciousness is not known in the reflection itself and so *for the reflective consciousness* it means neither the consciousness nor the content of consciousness.

26. The self-evident is to reflection a relation that *is* without being the content of a knowing that is known. "To know A is to know B" cannot be said to be no judgment and yet here we are not conscious of the problem of meaning its negation. It may well be that the assertion is a mistake but when it is made, it is made on the basis of an immediate unquestioning belief which is yet on the reflective level. The problem of meaning the negation of a perceived content does not arise during the perception because perception is not on the reflective level. But it is only reflectively that we say "to know A is to know B" and yet the knowledge here is immediate so that if later it turns out to be false, it is taken to be

an illusion and not merely a thinking error. Since the knowledge is reflectively immediate, there is not only no conscious problem of meaning its negation, there is the consciousness of such a problem not arising. It is only about what is known as the *content* of knowing that such a problem arises. So it is about judgment generally (which is on the reflective level) except what we take to be the primordial judgment, namely, "to know A is to know B." It is primordial judgment because it is the basis of necessary judgments that are the bases of all other judgments. A necessary judgment is still known mediately through the baffled attempt to conceive the opposite. This also is based on a judgment like "to know the inconceivability of the negation of a judgment is to know the judgment to be axiomatic." A judgment of the form "to know A is to know B" is self-evident judgment which is implied in all other judgments. That the terms of a judgment *have* a relation, that is, appear to be related to the relation only means that to know the terms is to know the relation—which is just a judgment of this form.

27. That the copula of this primordial self-evident judgment is not known as a content requires further explanation. The judgment is, indeed, knowledge and knowledge of the contents A and B as known, but so far as it is knowledge of the relation implied by the word "is," it is not knowledge of it as a content that is known. In the case of a judgment like "A is B," we understand the copula as a relation that is at least partially a content on a level with A and B. But in the judgment "to know A is to know B" the "is" is not on a level with the cognitions of A and B, far less with A and B. It is not known as known like the cognitions and their contents in the reflective consciousness. How then do we say that it is known? Because the sentence "to know A is to know B" is significant and what it signifies cannot be disbelieved. The import of the sentence or of the word "is" in it is, in fact, understood only when already spoken and not in the speaking of it. When even understood as already spoken, it is not retrospectively taken as the content of that speaking and *distinct from it*. It is understood, in fact, as *spoken* but not *as spoken of*. The word "is" in the judgment is not understood as known *content*.

28. What is understood (without disbelief) only as already spoken and not in the speaking of it is understood as known but not as known content. By "known content" is meant what is *knowable* as distinct from the knowing of it. It may not sometimes

be so known in the knowing of it but it may be known later. The import of the word "is" in the judgment "to know A is to know B" is not so knowable at all and may accordingly be (loosely) called a known no-content. It may be suggested that the import of the word "is" here, therefore, is the knowing act itself (or I) that is known by first appearing as content and then getting denied. It does not, however, appear at all as content to be negated: it is only symbolically spoken of later as content in the full consciousness that it is only verbally distinguished from the problematic knowing of it. Meantime the knowing of A and B that appears to reflection is definitely distinguished from it. What then the judgment "to know A is to know B" signifies is known but does not appear as content to be accepted or rejected. It appears neither as known knowing nor as the content of such knowing.

29. This judgment is the only self-evident entity of which reflection is aware and the copula in it is not only not known as content but is explicitly known as what known content—including the apparent reflective content "known knowing"—is not. The known position from which all content is distinguished—as represented by the copula here—is implied in all reflective knowledge, in all judgment like "A is B" where the "is" means this over and above a relation that is a content.

30. To sum up. In reflection on a content as known, the content implies knowing and is indefinitely distinct from it in the sense that it *means* this reference to knowing (though it means perfect distinction from knowing), that it does not mean independence of this reference and is not known as what is accidentally known. Reflection demands that it should be so known. The content is known to be only accidentally known, that is, to be only accidentally a content, when it is self-evident. The only self-evident of which we are reflectively aware is a judgment of the form "to know A is to know B" or what the word "is" in it stands for, this being meant in all judgments or knowledge on the reflective level. This then is the element in all that is reflectively known that is known as what need not be known, the element that is free from the implicational relation of the content to the knowing of it, the element that reflection demands to be isolated but cannot itself isolate. This is the absolute for knowing that demands to be freed from its immanence in the implicational distinction of content and knowing.

31. So far about knowing. We may now rapidly indicate how

the implicative relation of content and consciousness is demanded to be resolved in the case of willing and feeling. What implication of content and consciousness does reflective willing present? The willed content, as has been pointed out, is constituted by willing in the sense that apart from willing it is nothing at all. Yet the constituted content as definite in itself appears as a limitation to the constitutive willing: willing appears to be necessarily the willing of what is foreign to itself. In the reflective stage the willed content is appreciated as real through the willing but yet as its limitation, not as its self-limitation. It is not apparent at this stage that the will limits itself to realize itself, freely commits itself to a being to annul it and become freer. Reflection demands that the limit that is necessarily constituted by willing should be realized as self-limitation in this sense. That is how the implication of content and consciousness is problematically understood to be resolvable in the sphere of willing.

32. To elaborate the problem. The relation of two contents willed at once may be taken to suggest the relation between willed content and willing. Two contents, for example, two acts are said to be willed at once when one of them is a means to the other. Two unrelated acts cannot be said to be willed at once and two acts that are jointly means to a third act cannot be *distinctly* willed in the willing of the third act. A conscious will-relation of two contents must be a relation of prior and posterior, the prior being that through which the other is possible. In the relation of means and end as *willed*, the end is the prior through the willing of which it is possible to will a content *as means*. Now this relation of means and end has to be understood as the relation of willed content to willing. A willed act has to be taken as a means to the willing of it though it is through the willing that the willed act is possible. It is difficult to understand, however, how the willing of an act is the end of the act willed, how in other words willing is realized by the putting forth of the act, how one can be said to act in a particular way in order to act freely.

33. That we objectively act to be subjectively free, that the good will and nothing but the good will is the value for which we will an act—the view, in fact, of Kant—may be called the idealistic view in this connection. The realistic view here then would be that we act for an objective end and not for the subjective end of being free; and an extreme form of the view may be conceived that we objectively act in order that we may objectively act for evermore. In the case of knowing, we pointed out, the realistic

view is prima facie more acceptable than the idealistic view. In the case of willing apparently, the idealistic view is acceptable in the first instance. The realistic view amounts to saying that there is no willed act that is good in itself and the view that we objectively act in order that we may objectively act is just its logical consequence and its reductio ad absurdum. The idealistic view is consonant with the nature of reflective willing—namely, that the prior is the end, but in the reflective stage it appears to amount to the barren statement that it is good to will what it is good to will. The demand is to find a vital meaning for the statement, to understand how willing is a willing of itself.

34. Reflection indicates how it is to be understood. There is the difference between "I will this act" and "I will this act that I ought to will," when the former is not contrasted with the latter, the will-consciousness is expressible as an imperative "let this act be done." When, however, it is contrasted, it is expressed as mere information "I am doing it" while the latter is properly expressed as an imperative "let this be done" which implies "I may not do it." In contrast with it, the former appears as a statement of fact though by itself it appears as an imperative. The implication is that willing as represented by the former is itself a being that is to be superseded by willing as represented by the latter, that what is taken as free is implicitly not free, that therefore we will an act in order to get rid of the being of the act, get rid of the self-complacent will to continue in this being—what may be called the will to indolence. Reflection indicates the way but cannot understand willing or freedom at its limit.

35. In reflective feeling there is the definite consciousness of an indefinite distinction of the content felt and the feeling of it. The content felt is not definite in itself like the known or willed content and is understood in reference to this indefinite distinction definitely appearing to reflection *as though* it were a unity. We say "as though," because the unity does not appear as a definite self-subsistent unity from which its constituents are distinguishable. The implication of content and consciousness would be resolved in the sphere of feeling, if a unity of this kind could be apprehended. In the feeling of two contents together, we can reflectively apprehend a self-subsistent unity. Reflection accordingly demands such a unity of felt content and feeling but cannot itself understand it.

36. To explain. In the apprehension of an object having spatial

parts as beautiful, both the whole and the parts are felt but differently. The whole as a known content is distinct in itself and even if it be conceivably distinguished *from* the parts, the parts *as in the whole* cannot be distinguished from the whole and, therefore, can only be imperfectly distinguished from one another. The parts are, however, distinguished in the feeling way from the whole, being, in fact, felt as not felt in the way the whole is felt. The whole is felt to be beautiful but the parts are felt to be indifferent, felt to be "only known," such feeling of their mere knownness being necessary for the appreciation of the beauty of the whole. To feel two contents at once then is to feel their unity and to feel them otherwise than the unity. We try to understand the relation of the felt content and the feeling of it on this analogy. They appear imperfectly distinct and unity means to reflection an imperfect distinction of the constituents. But the unity does not appear to reflection self-subsistent in the sense of the constituents being distinguishable from it. Such a self-subsistent unity is, however, demanded.

37. As in the case of knowing and willing, so here one may imagine an alternation of realistic and idealistic or objectivistic and subjectivistic views. The unity of felt content and feeling may be understood as content that is indefinitely other than consciousness or as consciousness that is indefinitely other than the content. Value may be regarded as a kind of object though not as completely distinct from the consciousness of it as the known object or it may be taken to be an impersonalized feeling as somehow expressed in the object and thus objectified symbolically but not as a known character. Neither view appears to have any advantage over the other. Does reflection, however, indicate how consciously the alternation may be stopped and the unity come to be definite in itself?

38. Taking value, the unity of felt content and feeling, realistically as objective, we are reflectively aware of the value as referred to the known object that is distinguishable from it. We feel the object as known to be not the value, to be neutral, felt otherwise than the value. This is *feeling* the distinction of the object from the value of it and it is thus that the value tends to appear distinct in itself by having the object distinguished from it. So also if we take the value as an impersonalized feeling rather than as an objective character, in understanding it as expressed in the object we may

feel the knowing of the object as somehow *inside* the impersonal feeling, involved in it without being confused with it, much as the image in a mirror shows the mirror to be unaffected by it. Thus we may be said to be aware of the felt object as well as of the individual feeling as distinct from their unity.

39. So far the relation of felt content and feeling appears to be similar to the relation of two contents of the same feeling. In both there seems to be a unity from which its constituents are felt to be distinct. There is, however, discrepancy in an important respect. In appreciating a beautiful object where we feel the object as a whole as well as the parts, the parts that appear neutral are *together* felt to be distinct from the whole that appears beautiful. The beautiful object as beautiful thus appears in feeling as a whole isolated not only from other objects but also from its own knowable parts and thus shines as a self-subsistent something in the air. We cannot understand such a thing about the unity of content and consciousness called value. The felt content and the feeling consciousness are only *alternately* distinguished from the value that is their unity. The demand is for them *together* to be feelingly distinguished from value so that it may shine in isolation as a self-subsistent unity. To put it more correctly, the demand is for the concept of a value that is independent of valuation, of its reference to a known object. Reflection understands the problem but does not see the solution.

40. In all these cases then, reflection tries to understand the relation of the content of a mode of consciousness to the consciousness on the analogy of the relation of the contents of the same consciousness and finds that the analogy can be definitely extended only halfway, although it can indicate the way in which the indefinite aspect that remains over could conceivably be defined. In the case of knowing, how the known content could be without being known is not reflectively understood although the consciousness of the self-evident as distinct from the evident is consciousness of such a *possibility*. In the case of willing, it is reflectively indefinite how willing is the end of the act willed but the consciousness of the *ought* is consciousness of the possibility of getting rid of the being of the act willed. In the case of feeling, value should be understood but cannot be reflectively understood as the definite self-subsistent unity of felt content and feeling, but there is the consciousness of its possibility in the

reflective appreciation of a beautiful object as what "never was on sea or earth," isolated from its knowable relations not only to other objects but also to its own parts.

41. In all these cases, again, it will be noticed that what demands to be understood cannot actually be understood because such understanding would involve a species of negation that to reflection is unmeaning. In the case of knowing a known content has to be understood as what need not be content of any knowing. In the case of willing, the reality of willing has to be understood as the negation of being, of the being even of the content that is willed. In the case of feeling, the being of value has to be understood by the known as such being distinguished from it. To reflection, for the known content to be without being known is for it to be intrinsically unrelated to knowing in the way of distinction or identity. To be conscious of A and B, not to be able to deny either and yet to say they are utterly unrelated is apparently to state a contradiction. So to understand the willed act to be distinct from willing and yet to be nothing apart from it, or—to put it differently—for the act not to *be* and yet to be real as willing is to conceive the negation of an emergent distinct or the emergent distinction of a negation. To take the felt value also as a being from which known being is distinct is to be definitely conscious of an indefinite, to entertain without disbelief an *appearance* or an indifference of being and non-being. All the three—unrelatedness, negation of the emergent or the emergence of negation, and the indifference of being and non-being—imply unmeaning modes of negation to reflection; and yet the specifiable indefiniteness in the content of reflection demands to be defined precisely through such modes of negation. To admit the absolute in any form is to admit a negation that is unintelligible to the logic of the understanding.

42. The absolute may be generally defined from the standpoint of reflection as what is free from the implicational dualism of content and consciousness. There are three ways in which this freedom can be understood. The content may be freed from its reference to consciousness, that is, from its contenthood. Or consciousness may be freed from its reference to content, in which case it ceases to be conscious of anything beyond itself. Or the implicational relation itself may be freed from its terms as a definite self-subsistent unity. The known that is free from its

contenthood is known as the content that need not be content, is the self-evident *is*, just what we call *truth*—the absolute for knowing. Consciousness that is free from its content (in the sense that it solely constitutes its content, makes the content a content, creates its distinction from itself) is *freedom* of the will—the absolute for willing. The implicational relation of content and consciousness that is freed from their distinction as a unity is *value* in itself—the absolute for feeling.

43. Truth, freedom, and value then are absolutes for knowing, willing, and feeling. It is impossible to avoid this triple formulation of the absolute though the notion that there are three absolutes would be just as illegitimate as the notion of there being only one absolute. The absolute is not a *known content*, about which alone the question "one or many" has meaning. Truth is self-evident and is as such known but is no content; of value as the self-subsistent unity of content and consciousness, we cannot say either that it is not known or that it is like truth self-evident and, therefore, is no content; and there is no question even of knowing freedom, the belief in freedom being, as Kant pointed out, no intuition but willing itself. It is meaningless therefore to cognitively assert that there are three absolutes or one absolute. The absolute has, however, to be formulated in this triple way. Each is absolute but what are here understood as *three* are only their verbal symbols, they themselves being understood together but not *as together*.

44. For freedom, an alternative name would be reality. The real is understood either as will or what is given to will. Will means free will or freedom which though not theoretically known is not disbelieved, the belief in willing being willing itself. The expression of willing is always an imperative "let this be done," which means no known being and, if anything, means "let this known situation here be negated, *used* as means, melted into the future." Willing in this sense is the negation of being and is yet real, its reality consisting in the supersession of being. This comes out more explicitly in the consciousness of the imperative as the moral *ought*. *Ought* is real as the explicit rejection of the *is* or the actual that is known, explicit annulment of the known being of the presupposed "natural willing." Known being may be real but reality is understood in its purity as the conative rejection of

known being; or more accurately, since everything has to be understood here in conative terms, as the freedom to withdraw or abstain from "natural willing." Natural willing, called "natural" in reference to the *ought,* is in itself an imperative: the person who wills says to himself "let this be done" and not "I am doing it." So any willing and specially the willing to abstain from willing is unknowable freedom or reality. What is given to the will is also said to be real because either it is consumed by the will as a means to itself as end or if it cannot be so consumed, it has to be taken as an opposed will. Freedom or reality may accordingly be taken as synonymous.

45. Freedom or reality then is not known or, in other words, it is meaningless to call it truth. The true is the self-evident, that of which we are conscious as known but not as known content. Freedom or willing is not known at all or if we are aware of knowing it, we are aware of its knownness as illusory. We are only aware in one grade of willing that a presupposed willing of another grade—natural willing, as we have called it—had an illusory being or appeared to be known. What is known, however, may be either the self-evident in its purity or some relation of *given* contents—meaning contents given *to the will*—with the form of self-evidence. Every judgment, as has been pointed out, involves a self-evident judgment of the form "to know A is to know B." The self-evident in its purity is eternal truth and not reality: but a relation of given contents is not only said to be true but cannot also be said to be not real.

46. The real then is not true but the true may be real. So speaking of truth and value, we may say that truth is not value but value is not untrue. Just as the predicates true and false do not apply at all to freedom or reality, so the predicates valuable or worthless do not apply to truth. Truth is not felt or if it is felt, it is felt as unfelt, that is, as no value. But the predicate false applies to value insofar as the falsity of a felt value is denied though its truth cannot therefore be asserted. A value like beauty is evident but not self-evident; it appears as a content to an appreciative consciousness and appears without being disbelieved as an illusion but not as what need not have reference to the consciousness. The self-evident is the true and the evident is true if it implies self-evidence and till the self-evidence becomes explicit, it cannot be said to be false.

47. Again in respect of reality and value it may be said that while the predicates real and unreal do not apply to value, reality or freedom cannot be said not to be a value. Value is a felt being and is neither given to willing not is itself willed into existence though it may appear as the fulfillment of willing. It is in this respect similar to truth which may shine out in fulfillment of willing in the form of attention but is not brought into existence through its causality. Reality or freedom may, however, be felt and an act that is claimed to be willed is at least not morally indifferent if it is felt to have been genuinely willed. An act, in fact, that is felt to be morally indifferent is *eo ipso* felt to have been not free, not willing at all, the sole proof of freedom being in the retrospective moral valuation. To say that an act is free is to take it as not valueless though it may be going too far to assert that freedom is a value. Value is a felt *being* while freedom or willing is felt as the real *negation* of a known being and can at best be the felt being of a negation (of known being).

48. Thus it appears to be meaningless to speak of truth as a value, of value as real, or of reality as true while we can significantly speak of value as not false, of reality as not valueless, and of truth as not unreal, although we cannot positively assert value to be truth, reality to be value, and truth to be reality. Each of them is absolute and they cannot be spoken of as one or many. In one direction their identity and difference are alike meaningless and in another direction their identity is intelligible though not assertable. Truth is unrelated to value, value to reality, and reality to truth while value may be truth, reality value, and truth reality. The absolute may be regarded in this sense as an *alternation* of truth, value, and reality.

Bibliography of Bhattacharyya's Writings

"Studies in Vedantism." Calcutta: Calcutta University Press, 1907. P.R.S. Thesis, 1901.

"Some Aspects of Negation." Read before the Calcutta Philosophical Society, 1914, published that year.

"Place of the Indefinite in Logic." *Calcutta University Silver Jubilee Volume.* Serampore: Narayani Press, 1916.

"Definition of Relation as a Category of Existence." Unpublished essay, written in 1918.

"Sankara's Doctrine of Maya." *Proceedings* of the First Session of the Indian Philosophical Congress, 1925.

"Artistic Enjoyment." Unpublished essay, written in 1925.

"The Beautiful and the Ugly." Unpublished essay, written in 1925.

"The Jaina Theory of Anekantavada." First published in 1925; published again in *Jaina Antiquary*, 1943 (vol. 9, no. 1).

"Knowledge and Truth." Presidential Address, Section of Metaphysics, Indian Philosophical Congress, 1927. *Philosophical Quarterly*, April 1928.

"The Subject as Freedom." The Indian Institute of Philosophy, Amalner (Bombay), 1930.

"Prof. K. C. Bhattacharyya's Reply." *Philosophical Quarterly*, January 1932.

"Correction of Error as a Logical Process." Read before the Calcutta Philosophical Society, 1931. *Calcutta Review*, May 1931.

"The False and the Subjective." Read before the Calcutta Philosophical Society, 1932. *Calcutta Review*, October 1932.

"The Absolute and Its Alternative Forms." Presidential Address at the Poona Session of the Indian Philosophical Congress, 1933-1934.

"The Concept of Value." *Philosophical Quarterly*, January 1934.

"Lectures on Kant." Delivered before the Calcutta Philosophical Society, 1935-1936. Unpublished.

"The Concept of Philosophy." In *Contemporary Indian Philosophy*, London: George Allen Unwin, Ltd., 1936.

"The Advaita and Its Spiritual Significance." In *The Cultural Heritage of India*, Sri Ramkrishna Centenary Memorial, 1936.

"The Objective Interpretation of Percept and Image." *Philosophical Quarterly*, October 1936.

"Lectures on Sankya." Delivered at the Indian Institute of Philosophy, Amalner, 1937. Unpublished.

"Lectures on Yoga." Delivered at the Indian Institute of Philosophy, Amalner, 1937. Unpublished.

Index

About the Author

GEORGE BOSWORTH BURCH, now deceased, was Fletcher Professor of Philosophy, Emeritus, at Tufts University. He traveled extensively in Europe, Africa, and Asia, and on several occasions taught in India as a visiting professor.

Dr. Burch's introduction to this volume is based on thorough research in India, and when originally published was hailed as the best article ever to be written on Bhattacharyya and as an outstanding scholarly achievement. It remains unmatched and is, in fact, the only full treatment of this philosopher by any Western scholar.

Other books by Dr. Burch include a translation of *The Steps of Humility*, by Bernard, Abbot of Clairvaux, published by Harvard University Press in 1940; *Early Medieval Philosophy*, Columbia University Press, 1951; *The Divine Marriage* by Kalidasa, translated from the German, L. Verry, 1970; and *Alternative Goals in Religion: Love, Freedom, Truth*, McGill-Queen's University Press, 1972.